D0560653

In the Stillness of Quiet Moments

Emilie Barnes

HARVEST HOUSE PUBLISHERS
EUGENE, OREGON

Some devotional material adapted from Emilie Barnes' *You Are My Hiding Place*, copyright © 2009; *Meet Me Where I Am, Lord*, copyright © 2006; *Minute Meditations for Healing and Hope*, copyright © 2003.

Cover by Left Coast Design, Portland, Oregon

Cover photo © Shutterstock/Natu

IN THE STILLNESS OF QUIET MOMENTS
Copyright © 2012 by Emilie Barnes
Published by Harvest House Publishers
Eugene, Oregon 97402
www.harvesthousepublishers.com

ISBN 978-0-7369-4742-8 (pbk.)
ISBN 978-0-7369-4743-5 (eBook)

Printed in China

12 13 14 15 16 17 18 19 20 / KB-FC / 10 9 8 7 6 5 4 3 2 1

Seeking the Stillness

*M*y friend, imagine living a day without revisiting worries of yesterday or contemplating the potential concerns of tomorrow. Imagine shaping moments of quiet to experience God's peace and His leading. In God's presence, you can experience the deep comfort, the expansive hope, and the freeing grace of His love.

Often we have the intention of starting our day with the Lord in the stillness of the morning hours before our children clamber down the stairs searching for lost homework or we gather our belongings and head off to a full day of work, appointments, and commitments. But it doesn't happen.

Instead of a "ready, set, go" preparation for the day, most of us wake up to "Go! Go! Go!" In a split second, our minds and bodies are forced to transition from dreamland to the intense demands of a busy life. No wonder we often go through our routines feeling as though we're catching up or running in place. There is hope for us!

Preparing Your Heart

I invite you to change the pace of your day. Prepare a place in your life, your house, and your heart for inspirational quiet times with God. This is a "come as you are" invitation, by the way. Don't consider how this would be great if only you had more time, if only you were more spiritual, if only you believed quiet times for busy women were actually possible. I have good news. Peaceful, sacred moments with God can be part of *every* life. I can honestly say that such times *should* be a part of every life because we all need time to connect with our Creator. And our heavenly Father is eager for one-on-one sessions with you.

What we each bring with us to our quiet times will be different because we have unique burdens, worries, responsibilities, and needs. We might be experiencing very different seasons. For instance, when I share about a difficult physical journey I went through, if you haven't gone through that specifically, I know you've had to persevere through your own land of tears or times of transition. This is exactly why entering a tender, quiet time with God is so refreshing and healing.

In the past, you may have tried to create a place in your day and heart for stillness before the Lord. Or maybe you've only wished such a time was part of your routine. Today you can give yourself the life-changing gift of establishing time for quiet moments with your Creator and the Lover of your heart.

Find a comfy chair, an alcove with a window seat, or a porch swing with a front-row view of the yard and sky. You not only deserve this time, your heart is longing for this openness and wonder before the Lord.

Spend time with these brief devotions and in prayer. You'll discover a place and space of renewal and recharging, dreams and direction, becoming and belonging. Welcome, my friend!

Emilie

Knowing God in Stillness

Be still, and know that I am God.
PSALM 46:10 NIV

In this overstimulated world, do we even bother to listen for stillness, quietness, or silence? Do we take moments for reflection and rest so we can clear our heads and talk to God? For some people who have become addicted to noise, the sound of silence is very uncomfortable. They become uneasy or nervous. They need sounds—loud sounds. They want to mask the thoughts that rise up or the worries that might surface if they spend time in silence. Try telling a teenager (and most adults) to stop listening to their iPods or to turn off the television. They'll get upset, frustrated, and even angry.

Our culture is missing out on something great and important. Quiet times are refreshing to the soul, offering us reflection, a chance to mourn or be happy, and special opportunities to hear God speak to us in His still, small voice. Do such times exist in your home? Or is your house filled with the discordant sounds of television and pop music? Is it any wonder that many of us don't know how to cultivate silence? Consequently, we can't teach it to our children, either. Our hearts are longing for such peace, but we cover up that desire with more noise, more activity, and more distractions.

Perhaps your children are already well on the road to the addiction to noise—the need for constant audio activity. If so, you will be shortchanging them by not teaching them the joys of silence and the treasure of prayer.

The psalmist knew that to know God we have to stop striving and become still. The business of life must come to a halt if we want to become more intimate with God.

· · · · ·

God of peace, I find myself anxious. Help me establish a quiet time each day so I can be still. In this stillness, let me ponder who You are. I want to know You in a greater way. Give me the courage to establish my home as a place of peace, not audio discord. Amen.

That Inner Feeling

The LORD has done what He purposed;
He has accomplished His word.

LAMENTATIONS 2:17

The older I become, the more I realize that living from my heart has value. I don't want to get into the trap of following everyone else because it's the group thing to do. I want to live a life that is meaningful to me and my family. I want my decisions to be based on my Christian values not on what TV, Madison Avenue, and popular newsstand magazines tell me.

To live intuitively, we must have some quiet time to read and think. Hectic lives don't permit us to hear the heartbeat of our souls. When we are too busy, we don't have time to dwell on the important issues in life. I find that when I'm rushed, I have an inner disturbance that prevents me from making well-thought-out decisions. When you and I are hurried, we have a tendency to harbor deep anger inside because we forget to set time aside for ourselves. Our personal growth comes to a standstill.

Life can present you with times of waiting when you face illness, caregiving, a trial, or even seasons of anticipating a great joy or change. But before you face such things, let yourself be directed to times of stillness before the Lord. Dwell on what your heart knows to be true, and you will discover a greater sense of God's love and purpose for you.

* * * * *

Father, let me be more aware of the feelings of my heart. You have given me so many of the desires of my heart. I want to be more sensitive to what You are teaching me about life. I search for the solitude of peace and tranquility so I can hear Your thoughts. Amen.

Faith Is a Gift

Now faith is the assurance of things hoped for,
the conviction of things not seen.

HEBREWS 11:1

*D*o you have trouble believing in something you haven't seen? Jesus' disciple Thomas did. He said he wouldn't believe in Jesus' resurrection until he actually saw and touched the Lord.

Jesus told Thomas, "Because you have seen me, you have believed; blessed are those who have not seen and yet have believed" (John 20:29 NIV). I don't believe Jesus was scolding Thomas when He said this. He was just saying that Thomas would be a lot happier—that's what "blessed" means!—if he could learn to take some things on faith.

I think that's true for many of us. We have faith, and yet we keep asking for proof or more clarification. God doesn't reprimand us because of this. He lovingly reveals Himself time after time. However, we are missing out on the abundance of lives lived in absolute faith when we question more than we rest in God's peace.

What is so incredible is that every day I take it on faith that my car will start, my TV will click on, my Internet server will function. How all these things work is a mystery to me, but they do—at least most of the time. So if I can manage to believe in these man-made "miracles," why should I have trouble believing in God and His divine miracles? Though I haven't physically seen Him, I have felt God's presence. I have seen His works. As a result, I no longer waste my energy fussing over whether God is real. Instead, I choose to enjoy the blessings of belief.

* * * * *

Lord, I'm so thankful I have not let the world blind my eyes to You. You are here even amid all the smoke screens of life. I know You are here even though I can't see You. Amen.

Think Positively

Whatever is true, whatever is honorable, whatever is right, whatever is pure, whatever is lovely, whatever is of good repute, if there is any excellence and if anything worthy of praise, dwell on these things.

PHILIPPIANS 4:8

An old Chinese proverb states, "What we think, we are." That is so true. Our thought processes determine who we are. If we think lustful thoughts, we become lustful. If thoughts of anger enter our minds, we become angry. What we think is what we begin to feel. Anger, stress, lust, bitterness, and unhappiness have a way of weaseling into our minds and creating patterns of negativity. We increase our stress and frustration with life when we constantly dialog with ourselves by saying "I hate my job," "I don't like Mary," "This place is always a mess," "I hate being married," "No one ever helps me with the chores," and "This job is lousy." If we continue these mental conversations, we internalize the negative beliefs, which is very destructive to our lives.

To nip these attacks in the bud, we need to pursue positive thoughts, especially those mentioned in today's Scripture. We choose which road we will travel—one that spirals downward or one that spirals upward into a more healthy environment. The apostle Paul tells us to think on things that are:

- true
- honorable
- right
- pure
- lovely
- good repute
- whatever is excellent and worthy of praise

This is certainly contrary to what the world tells us to do. We must make a conscious effort to think in these godly terms. When we do, our whole world will change. These thoughts will give us new criteria for what we read, view, listen to, eat, and think. We will find many riches, and the stresses of life will be greatly reduced.

* * * * *

Father God, You have given me only one life to live, and I certainly want it to reflect my love for You. Give me the strength to make the best choices for my mind, body, and soul. I want to travel the road less traveled—the road to You. Amen.

Surviving the Storm

The righteous person may have many troubles,
but the LORD delivers him from them all.

PSALM 34:19 NIV

In the past few years we have all witnessed, if not experienced, some very traumatic storms and natural disasters. It grieves us when people face such devastation. We strive to do what we can to help those who have lost homes, loved ones, or hope. With this is mind, it is good for us to remember that not every storm faced is literal. During our lifetimes, all of us will experience storms that are as devastating as the tragedies of tornados, floods, hurricanes, and fires. They may not be as evident as a physical storm, but when we experience them, they are just as real to us. Such tumults can turn our lives around. They can turn our dreams into nightmares. Some of these storms are called divorce, disease, death, betrayal, bankruptcy, abuse, adultery, and all types of addictions.

What do we do when these difficulties hit our lives? God has us covered. As we pray and seek His guidance, we are to go to Scripture and embrace what He has to say about our circumstances, lives, direction, and needs, both great and small. Prepare your heart for the storms ahead by becoming familiar with God's Word. Remember, God has a purpose for our lives: "We know that God causes all things to work

15

together for good to those who love God, to those who are called according to His purpose" (Romans 8:28).

And we have God's presence to comfort us too. In the Gospels we read that Jesus was with each person in the storm. He did not leave them alone. In each of our storms He is with us: "Peace I leave with you; My peace I give to you; not as the world gives do I give to you. Do not let your heart be troubled, nor let it be fearful" (John 14:27).

We also have God's power: "God has not given us a spirit of timidity, but of power and love and discipline" (2 Timothy 1:7).

How will we respond when the storms occur? Don't look down and don't look back. Instead, look upward toward the heavens and ask God to give you a new vision and purpose for this event. In our family, when the storms come crashing into our lives, we ask God, "What lesson are You trying to teach us in this experience?"

And don't keep what you learn from the storms to yourself. Be available and willing to help others as they stand against their storms of life. Always seek God's wisdom and strength when offering to help a loved one, a neighbor, or a stranger.

· · · · ·

Lord, show me Your purpose for each of my storms. Let me learn something, otherwise those storms will be of little value for my life. From Scripture and from experience I know You are always with me. Thank You! Amen.

The Coming of Joy

*Though the fig tree does not bud and there
are no grapes on the vines, though the olive
crop fails and the fields produce no food...
yet I will rejoice in the LORD,
I will be joyful in God my Savior.*

HABAKKUK 3:17-18 NIV

True joy does not come from material possessions, even though they can be wonderful. It does not come from having a healthy family or a successful career, although those can be meaningful and fulfilling. It doesn't come from physical pleasure or delighting the senses. All these things can be good, but eventually they will be gone. Real joy—the kind that lasts forever—comes from steadfast trust in the Lord.

Through good times and bad times, through sickness and health, through all sorts of ups and downs, we can still express honest joy because we belong to God, because He has ultimate control over what happens to us, and because we trust Him to make all things work together for our good. The apostle Paul sets the example in Philippians 4:11: "I have learned how to get along happily whether I have much or little" (TLB).

* * * * *

Father God, let my joy be complete in You. I have tasted victory and defeat, and in all situations Your joy radiates in my heart. May those around me see the joy You give me. Amen.

The Making of a Home

Unless the LORD builds the house,
they labor in vain who build it.
PSALM 127:1

Do you sometimes feel that your house has just become a place to repair broken objects, mow the lawn, pay off the mortgage, serve quick meals, and put in a few hours of sleep each night? There was a time when my home felt just like that. But finally I figured out that a real home is much more. It's a place where people live, grow, laugh, cry, learn, and create together. I love the concept behind this little quote. After watching his house burn down, a small child said, "We still have a home. We just don't have a house to put it in." He understood what a home really is.

Our homes should be grace centers for the whole family. We don't have to be perfect—just forgiven. Our homes are places where we can nurture and be ourselves. We all need a place to be just us, with no pretense needed. We can laugh when we feel like it and cry when we need to. We can make mistakes, we can agree, and we can disagree. Home should be places where happy experiences occur—places sheltered from the problems of the world. Places of love, acceptance, security, and faith. When we read the morning newspaper, we are confronted with the tragedies around us. We realize the world outside our front door is falling apart, but within our four walls we can offer a place called home.

What can we do to have homes like God intended? As with everything in life, when something is broken we go back to the instruction manual. In this case, it's the Bible. The home is God's idea—not something invented by people. In the original plan of creation, God designed the home to be the foundation of society—a place to meet the mental, spiritual, physical, and emotional needs of people.

Marriage is not a temporary convenience to be maintained as long as it feels good. God designed the family as an enduring relationship in which, with His care, humans can weather the storms of life together. The home is God's loving shelter for growing to maturity.

God is not only the designer, but He also wants to take the headship of family life. He wants to guide and give love, peace, and forgiveness abundantly. We've got our work cut out for us if we want a true home. We must live life with a big purpose—to have not just a house but a home.

• • • • •

Father God, You know I want my house to be more than just a place. I want it to be a home. I want to yield to Your leadership. Give me wisdom, understanding, and knowledge. Amen.

"Always" Means Always

[Love] always protects, always trusts,
always hopes, always perseveres.
1 CORINTHIANS 13:7 NIV

Sometimes it's hard for us mere mortals to under-stand the word "always." In today's culture we don't understand love as that kind of commitment. When we say "always," don't we usually mean "sometimes"…or "most of the time"? But "always" really means eternal and everlasting. Can we really commit to always?

When God, through Scripture, says "always," He means always with no exceptions. Never changing, dependable for eternity. I am challenged when the apostle Paul says that love…

- ❧ always protects
- ❧ always trusts
- ❧ always hopes
- ❧ always perseveres

I so want my husband and children to honor me with that kind of love. I want to be a woman who is known for her word: "When Mom says something, you can take it to the bank." In this regard, my advice is, "Do what you say you are going to do." By so doing, you teach your children the meaning of being trustworthy. You also teach them to trust others—and that's a rare quality in this age of cynicism. I've learned that the person who trusts others makes fewer mistakes than the person who distrusts.

Romans 8:24 says, "We are saved by trusting. And trusting means looking forward to getting something we don't yet have—for a man who already has something doesn't need to hope and trust that he will get it" (TLB).

We are people of integrity. Our word can always be trusted. When we are women like this, our husbands, our children, and our friends will rise and bless us (Proverbs 31:28).

* * * * *

Almighty God, I want to be an "always" person. When I say something, I want it always to be true. I want people to be able to say with certainty, "If she said it, it must be true." Help me be this kind of woman. Amen.

Relief and Restoration

*[Jesus said,] "Come to me, all you who are weary and
burdened, and I will give you rest."*
MATTHEW 11:28 NIV

I enjoy the process of restoring old furniture and dec-
orative items. With a little paint or varnish, a yard or
two of fabric, and a little creative imagination, almost any
worn-out item can be restored to beauty or usefulness. There
is such joy in watching that transformation take place.

When I feel broken and worn, I wonder if my heavenly
Father finds the same kind of joy in restoring me. Why?
Because restoration is exactly what He promises us in Scrip-
ture. "He restores my soul," sings the psalmist (Psalm 23:3).
"The God of all grace, who called you to His eternal glory in
Christ, will Himself perfect, confirm, strengthen and estab-
lish you," says Peter (1 Peter 5:10).

Throughout His earthly ministry, Jesus restored physical health, spiritual health, even physical life…and passed
that restorative power on to His followers through the Holy
Spirit. When illness strikes, when experiences knock us low,
when life leaves us wounded, our natural heart-cry to our
heavenly Father is the cry of a child: "Please make it better."
And He does just that. I believe this with all my heart!

Every one of us has benefited from the normal healing
processes built into creation. And these natural processes are

truly miraculous. I am astonished by the ways cells work to close a wound, knit a broken bone together, and combat an infection. I'm amazed at the way the human mind can adapt and move forward after a disappointment or crushing tragedy. I am astounded by the resilience of the human spirit, the way people can rebound from a setback to go on to live creative and positive lives. Healing is built into the very design of the world.

I believe God also works through humans to do His restorative work. Traditional and alternative doctors can be agents of remarkable healing, and so can ministers, therapists, counselors, and all those with the spiritual gift of healing. And so can loving family and friends who pour their energies into prayer and practical help.

Healing can take many forms. Watch for and take note of the many ways God brings healing and wholeness to your life. I'm sure you will discover and experience deep gratitude and peace along the way.

· · · · ·

Dear God of all grace, thank You for looking at my brokenness with the eye of a restorer and the heart of a creator. There is no heartache, hardship, or loss that cannot be turned into hope and faith through Your loving touch. Amen.

Waiting for Restoration

Take my yoke upon you and learn from me,
for I am gentle and humble in heart, and
you will find rest for your souls.
MATTHEW 11:29 NIV

Restoration is not always instantaneous. But God is God. Our loving, redemptive Father's restoration proceeds on His timetable and according to His priorities. By the Lord's mercy, we are being healed, being made perfect in a process that will take our entire lifetimes…and perhaps even longer…to complete. We can feel the gentle touch of God's comfort, soft as a mother's kiss, on our hearts. This is a quiet reminder that He is still here, and the calm He provides keeps us going.

God brings beauty out of brokenness and gently guides us into wholeness and maturity. How can we not trust Him to finish the job in us? Healing is intended to be a partnership. God does the restoration, yes, but we are not passive. We are *expected* to respond and participate in the process by following God's plan for our lives, keeping our hearts open to Him, learning more about how He works, and offering Him our hearts. We need to stay close to Him by reading the Scriptures, spending time in prayer, heeding His Word about what our part is in our healing, and, most importantly, obeying Him.

Here on earth, the restoration we experience is ongoing and truly miraculous, but also partial and problematic. Here on earth the very process of healing leaves us marked and scarred (not to mention wrinkled and sagging). In the end, though, the healing we are promised is whole and complete. When God is through with us, we will be more real than we ever thought possible—as well as unscarred and unwrinkled and energetic and full of life and love. I don't know about you, but I can't wait!

• • • • •

God, thank You for Your healing touch. You restore my soul to gladness. You give me rest in the midst of my trials and provide relief from my burdens. You are an amazing God. I love You. Amen.

Be a Woman of Good Character

*[Your beauty] should be that of your inner self, the
unfading beauty of a gentle and quiet spirit, which is
of great worth in God's sight.*

1 PETER 3:4 NIV

Even in hard financial times, many men and women seem to find ways to spend money—lots of money—on the maintenance and improvement of their physical appearance. What might be a better way to draw goodness from lean economic times is to shift our priorities and become more aware of what really matters. A perfect example is for us to enhance and radiate our inner beauty.

One sure way of instantly becoming more beautiful is by refusing to be a complainer. The least attractive person in a room, in a meeting, or in a line at the store is surely the one loudly expressing her problems or her grievances. We can still be charming even in very tough times. I have the privilege of knowing some very godly women who model their inward beauty to me. They are wonderful ladies to be around. They adorn themselves with a gentle and quiet spirit that is pleasing to the Lord. As I grow older, I want to be more lovely inside, keeping in mind that growing older brings me closer to being with my Lord in heaven.

All the products we see in commercials won't stop the aging process or bring back our youth. But God does promise a formula that will give us renewed strength:

> Though youths grow weary and tired, and vigorous young men stumble badly, yet those who wait for the LORD will gain new strength; they will mount up with wings like eagles, they will run and not get tired, they will walk and not become weary (Isaiah 40:30-31).

This is definitely a promise of spiritual vitality that defies the ravages of time! When we look to Scripture for truth, we can develop into the kind of women God created us to be—women of good character. His promises come alive when we put our trust in Him for strength of heart, energy for our souls, and vigor in our spirits.

* * * * *

Lord, keep me from concentrating on the outer part of my life, and help me develop the muscles of my inside person. Put blinders on my eyes when I view all the ads that suggest outward appearance makes a successful woman. Amen.

Inspiration for Your Quiet Moments

🐞 🐞 🐞

Prepare a Special Nook

*Y*ou will more easily commit to setting aside quiet moments if you create a nice place to enjoy the stillness. Nothing fancy is required. If you have a special chair or area of a room, take time to tidy it, clear it of anything that distracts or reminds you of to-do lists. Keep it free of clutter. Decorate with simple items that will help you savor your time of prayer. A candle, this devotional, your Bible, and even a photo or two of those you often pray for will be lovely.

This probably won't be a space that is off-limits to others during the day, so beforehand set aside just five minutes to clear it of any of your family's odds and ends so that it greets you with the simplicity of a refuge. This works especially well if you tidy up the night before and meet with God first thing in the morning.

A Gentle, Quiet Spirit

*"I know the plans I have for you," declares the LORD,
"plans to prosper you and not to harm you,
plans to give you hope and a future."*

JEREMIAH 29:11 NIV

*L*et me assure you that men love to be in the presence of a real lady. Such a woman makes men feel more masculine, more self-confident, and more relaxed. A real lady influences those around her with her gentle spirit instead of just how she looks and dresses. It is all about who she is. What do I mean by a "real lady"? A woman who worked in our local bank for years comes to mind. As she dealt with her customers, she radiated peace. She always offered tranquility, warmth, friendliness, courtesy, and a welcoming spirit.

What is "feminine"? It's not a particular style, form, dress, or interior decorating motif. Feminine encompasses an infinite variety of physical appearances. It is a softness, gentleness, and graciousness that men don't have. A woman can be the president of a corporation or be a tough and aggressive participant in the business world and still be feminine. To me, feminine also means that a woman has a sense of who she is apart from what she does. She nurtures a strong spirituality and manifests the fruit of the Spirit— love, joy, peace, forbearance, kindness, goodness, faithfulness, gentleness, and self-control in every aspect of her life (see Galatians 5:22-23 NIV). Femininity also brings to mind a deep concern for her husband and children, the maternal awareness that she is raising not only her children but the generations that follow. A truly feminine woman understands the gifts of being a godly wife and mother.

A gentle and quiet spirit, tranquility, being at peace, sharing the fruit of the Spirit with people—these qualities are a direct result of a woman's relationship with God. When a woman is right with God, she doesn't feel any need to prove herself. Confident in herself and aware of her God-given strengths, she doesn't feel compelled to use those strengths to control people. She enjoys an inner contentment that isn't based on accomplishments, status, authority, power, or other people's opinions.

· · · · ·

Father God, my heart gets heavy when I'm trying to be a woman outside that doesn't match who I am on the inside. I truly want a quiet and gentle spirit based on You. Give me the strength to soften my edges. Amen.

Give Prayer a Try

Because he bends down and listens,
I will pray as long as I breathe!

PSALM 116:2 TLB

Who has time to pray? My to-do list is always longer than my day. I run from the time the alarm goes off in the morning until I fall into bed at night. How can I possibly find time to do one more thing? When could I fit in even a few minutes to read the Bible or pray?"

I thought that way for many years, but finally I decided to make prayer one of my top priorities. I started to get up 30 minutes before the rest of the family each day, and I spent that time with God. The days I did this went so much smoother. I had more discipline and my emotional stability was much more even. I'm glad I established this habit in my life because when I face dark times now I already have a line of communication with my heavenly Father open. We became prayer partners long ago, and what an amazing blessing that has been! You can have this relationship and connection with God daily too.

Are you wondering what to talk to God about when you pray? Here are a few suggestions:

    ❧ Praise God for who He is—the Creator and
        Sustainer of the whole universe, yet someone who

is interested in each of us (Psalm 150; Matthew 10:30).

- ♆ Thank God for what He has done for you, for all He is doing for you, and for all that He will do for you (Philippians 4:6).

- ♆ Confess your sins. Tell God about the things you have done and said and thought for which you are sorry. God is "faithful and righteous to forgive us our sins" (1 John 1:9).

- ♆ Pray for your family and for friends and neighbors who have needs—physical and spiritual. Ask God to work in the heart of someone you hope will come to know Jesus as Savior. Pray for government officials, for your minister, and for missionaries and other Christian servants (Philippians 2:4).

- ♆ Pray for yourself. Ask for guidance for the day ahead. Ask God to help you do His will. Ask Him to arrange opportunities to serve Him throughout the day (Ephesians 1:17-18; James 1:5).

• • • • •

Lord, may I never forget to call on You in every situation. Amen.

The Spirit of Femininity

Your heart was lifted up because of your beauty.

EZEKIEL 28:17

When I was a little girl, I dreamed of being a lady. The world of *Little Women*, with its gracious manners and old-fashioned, flowing dresses, fascinated me. Softness and lace, tantalizing fragrance, exquisite textures, nurturing spirits, and a love of beauty—these images of femininity shaped my earliest ideas of loveliness.

Is that kind of femininity a lost value today? I don't believe it. The world has changed, and most of us work and play in simple shirts or business suits or jeans instead of flowing gowns. But I still believe that somewhere in the heart of most of us is a little girl who longs to be a lady.

I also believe that today's world is hungering to be transformed by the spirit of femininity. What better antidote for an impersonal and violent society than warm, gentle, feminine strength? What better cure for cluttered lives than love of beauty and confidence in our ability to make things lovely? What better hope for the future than a nurturing mother's heart that is more concerned for the next generation than for its own selfish desires? All these qualities—gentle strength, love of beauty, care, and nurturing—are part of the spirit of femininity.

The gift of our femininity is something we can give to ourselves and to the people around us. Just one flower or one candle can warm a cold, no-nonsense atmosphere. Women have always had the ability to transform an environment to make it comfortable and inviting. I believe we should rejoice in that ability and make the most of it.

The spirit of femininity is so many things. To me, it is represented by objects chosen for their beauty as well as their usefulness and lovingly cared for. It is people accepted and nurtured, loveliness embraced and shared. More important, the spirit of femininity is care and compassion. In my mind, the most feminine woman is one with an eye and ear for others and a heart for God.

* * * * *

Father, let my heart be opened to those things that reflect Your love to those people around me. I want to be a sweet fragrance to the world. Amen.

Self-talk

*How precious it is, Lord, to realize that you are
thinking about me constantly! I can't even
count how many times a day your thoughts turn
toward me. And when I waken in the morning,
you are still thinking of me!*

PSALM 139:17 TLB

o you ever catch your thoughts taking a negative
turn? When you check your self-talk, do you realize a lot of junk is crossing your mind? Most of us are very good at criticizing ourselves. We find fault very easily. I suggest that we develop a more positive thought process. When I know that God is thinking about me constantly, how can I not think more positively about myself? If I am worthy to Him, why should I not be worthy to me? As you look in the mirror of life, don't be afraid to say loud and clear, "Good job!" We aren't being conceited when we recognize the good in our lives; however, we must recognize that ultimately all good comes from our heavenly Father.

Many times, after I went through a delicate medical procedure, my Bob and I would celebrate by doing something special. Usually we didn't do anything big—just a recognition that I had done a "good job" by persevering and holding up.

Keep telling yourself the positives. Don't let the negatives take hold of your thoughts. And when you feel alone with your experiences or thoughts, remember you can't count the number of times the Lord is thinking of you because the number is so vast. He *never* leaves you. Hold on to that thought today with all of your heart.

●　●　●　●　●

Dear Lord, knowing that You are thinking of me has often given me strength to carry on for another day. Your thoughts are precious to me! Amen.

Make Time for a Garden

Teach us to number our days,
that we may gain a heart of wisdom.

PSALM 90:12 NIV

Spending time in nature is a way to experience the awesome sanctuary of the Lord. You'll be surprised how being with God in His splendid creation is like being in His sacred classroom. You'll discover His incredible attention to detail, His care for the cycles and seasons of life, His exquisite creativity, and His patience for everything to grow in its own time...including us.

You'll take in the beauty of buds and blooms, sprigs of green, and dangling clusters of purple. You can breathe in deeply, allowing the scent of lilacs, roses, and mint to fill you with delight. Step outside of your yard or garden, and the wonders just keep on coming. The fragrance of sweet peas and clematis might cover you as you walk around your neighborhood or at a local park.

Noticing creation's intricacies reminds us of God's precious care for each and every living thing. It beckons us to fill our hearts with joy and rid our minds of worries and complaints. There is refreshment for body, mind, and spirit when we take time to be outdoors and relax in God's playground. I find that I want to rejoice after a short time in the sunlight or in the presence of a majestic tree that reaches toward heaven. The fresh air makes my heart soar as I think of so many ways that God's miracles touch my life.

Those miracles are all around you and me. We just have to be willing and fortunate enough to notice them and be grateful. Take time to walk with God in your garden, beside a rushing river, or along a wooded trail. Meet God on this adventure and experience sweet communion with the Maker of such wondrous life.

· · · · ·

Father God, let me learn to slow down from my hectic pace of life. I so enjoy being around all of Your creation. Give me the desire and time to develop greenery in and around my home. Amen.

Be Thankful and Content

Bless the LORD, O my soul, and all that is within me,
bless His holy name. Bless the LORD, O my soul,
and forget none of His benefits.
PSALM 103:1-2

From the time they first utter words, we teach our children to say "thank you." When someone gives them a gift or compliment—and before they can even utter the words—we jump right in and remind them, "Now what do you say?" However, as we grow from childhood to adulthood, we often forget our manners and hold back from expressing our appreciation to someone who does us a service.

Sometimes we do the same thing when it comes to God. He loves to hear and know we are thankful for all He bestows on us. He is the provider of all we have!

> A person can do nothing better than to eat and drink
> and find satisfaction in their own toil. This too, I see,
> is from the hand of God, for without him, who can
> eat or find enjoyment? (Ecclesiastes 2:24-25 NIV).

Appreciative hearts give thanks. One way to express our thanks for our food is to give a blessing each time we have a meal. Our family always offers a blessing of grace before we eat. This is a tradition whether we're at home or at a restaurant. We never want to forget where our food comes from.

We always want to let God know that we appreciate His provision.

It is good to look back over this short life and realize how God has been faithful all along the way. He has always provided for our needs. Not necessarily for our wants, but always for our needs. The password for entering into God's presence is "thank You": "Enter His gates with thanksgiving and His courts with praise. Give thanks to Him, bless His name" (Psalm 100:4).

We humbly reach out to God with thanksgiving and praise. One of the leading indicators of our spiritual walk with God is our thankfulness for all He has done for us. The apostle Paul told us to be content in all situations (Philippians 4:11). When we are restless and find ourselves discontented with our lives and our situations, it's accentuated when we don't have a heart that chooses to give thanks.

* * * * *

God, don't let me forget to always be thankful for what You do for me. You are a gracious God who continually pours out blessings on my life. Thank You for everything—big and small. Amen.

Deepen Your Friendships

Love is very patient and kind, never jealous or
envious, never boastful or proud.
1 Corinthians 13:4 tlb

*F*or whatever reason, it's often not as easy for a man to
cultivate a friendship as it is for a woman. Further-
more, if your husband doesn't come from a very demonstra-
tive family, he may not have a good male role model for how
to be a friend to his male friends or even to you. You may
have to teach him how to be a friend. Here are five points
that may help you:

- Assign top priority to your friendships. How
  important are your friendships? How you spend
  your time will show you. Each of us does what we
  want to; very little gets in the way of doing what
  is most important to us. So consider again how
  important your friendships are to you. Make room
  and take time to develop good friends.

- Cultivate transparency in your relationships.
  When we are honest with ourselves about who we
  are (emotionally and otherwise), we can be better
  friends. Our willingness to be open about who we
  are encourages trust and openness on the part of

others. Be yourself in your openness. Just remember that what is shared in private stays private.

- Dare to talk about affection. When building that friendship with your husband, take a risk and show and share your love for your mate. One expression that Bob shares with me when he does a kind deed or gives me a hug is "Just another way to show that I love you!" Be willing to be open in your conversation about your affection for each other. Tell your mate what makes you feel good. It's okay to be shy and bashful and even to get embarrassed—but do it anyway.

- Give your mate freedom. Love is never oppressive or possessive. Let your mate be all that God wants him to be. That means in failure as well as in success. Your mate needs to be free from words that discourage and words that harm. Be a part of his dreams. Help give wings to his plans for the future. A friend is one who gives encouragement not a wet blanket. Give him the freedom to be himself. Encourage your husband to be the unique person God created him to be.

- Learn the language of love. Each of us needs to learn how to say "I love you." I'm not talking about only speaking out loud these three powerful words (although that's important to do). We need to also say "I love you" by showing our respect.

Certain rituals and traditions in our family enable us to express our love for one another. We kiss each other goodnight and say, "May God bless your sleep." We celebrate our love on anniversaries and birthdays by giving small gifts. We telephone one another when we're apart, visit favorite restaurants on special occasions, and so on. All of these things—spontaneous acts as well as carefully planned events—make for a special friendship.

• • • • •

Father God, help me broaden my friendship with my husband by considering and implementing these five guidelines. Show me how to gently share what true friendship is. Amen.

Harmony Grows at Home

*All of you be harmonious, sympathetic, brotherly, kind-
hearted, and humble in spirit... You were called for the
very purpose that you might inherit a blessing.*

1 PETER 3:8-9

When Bob and I were in Charleston, South Caro-
lina, we toured an old African-American craft dis-
trict. We ran across an apron that had "If Mama ain't happy,
no one is happy" embroidered on it. We realized that the
maker of this apron had captured the essence of marriage. In
a healthy marriage, both partners are happy in the roles they
play. When a spouse is happy and feels appreciated, he or
she wants to be of help to the other. If your mate is unhappy,
the last thing he wants to do is help you out or please you.

I recognize and acknowledge that you are not responsible for your husband's happiness; he alone is accountable for
that. However, we wives do play a large part in making our
mates feel appreciated. Don't take it for granted that your
husband is thoroughly aware that you are know all he does
for you. As a marriage partner, it's important that you take
the time to show and say that your mate is respected for all he
does for the family. In some cases, his boss at work gives little praise for his efforts, so your family's praises might be the
only positive affirmations he receives each day. As partners,
we want to treat our spouses as well as we do our close friends.

Bob and I genuinely share our appreciation for each other. We never take anything for granted. A little "thank you" goes a long way to show our mates that their efforts are noticed and valued. Make today a new beginning of loving and caring and serving in your marriage.

. . . . .

Father God, from the bottom of my heart I want my husband to know that he is appreciated and loved. I want to show him how much I like the things he does for me and our family. Let today be a new day in our lives. Show me how to let him know I notice and respect what he does. Amen.

His Name Has Honor

Lord, with all my heart I thank you.
I will sing your praises before the armies of angels.
I face your Temple as I worship, giving thanks
to you for all your loving-kindness and your
faithfulness, for your promises are backed by
all the honor of your name. When I pray,
you answer me and encourage me
by giving me the strength I need.
PSALM 138:2-3 TLB

When someone promises me something, I want to know what backs up that promise. Does he have enough financial resources to make that pledge? Does he have the political power to make that guarantee? Has he been a man of honor who has lived up to his word? Honor is one of our most valuable possessions. It takes years to obtain, but it can be lost in the twinkling of an eye.

God has demonstrated His abiding character and His commitment to keep His promises. When He gives us a promise in His Word, we can take it to the bank because it's sealed with His honor.

As I've walked through troublesome valleys, including battling cancer, I can definitely say that God lives up to every promise. He heard and answered my prayers. He's been my shield and protector. He has given me peace

47

beyond description. He has encouraged me by giving me the strength I needed for every difficult occasion.

Enter your time of quiet today with the full knowledge that God is listening to your every word. He sees your tears. He knows the potential joy of the dream that is just beginning to unfold in you. Just as the Lord provided me with strength on days when I wasn't sure how to step forward, He is with you to do the same in His remarkable way.

. . . . .

Father God, You are the God of every moment. Teach me to order my ways even as You direct my paths. Thank You for Your instructive presence in my life. Amen.

The Strength You Need

He gives strength to the weary, and to him
who lacks might He increases power.
ISAIAH 40:29

*A*re you always tired? As a busy mom, I yearned for rest and sleep. The activities of the day often seemed beyond my strength. At no other time in my life can I remember ever being so utterly drained of energy. Each day I looked forward to evening when I could tuck the children into bed and get some much-needed rest.

Looking back, I'm sure those days weren't much fun for my husband, Bob, either. When he came home from work, my energy had long since been sapped by the day's activities. By age 21, I was responsible for five children—our two and my brother's three children, whom Bob and I took in. Life at that time absolutely overwhelmed me. Later, after the children were grown, Bob and I were busy with our More Hours in My Day Ministry, and that too required a great deal of energy and time. It was a gift, just like parenting, because it required me to depend on God's strength every day.

When we have low physical reserves, we are open prey for the enemy. Satan can attack us with all sorts of accusations about our lot in life. His goal is to cause us to resent the demands made on us and to cast doubt on God's faithfulness.

But God knows our weaknesses, and in every case He will send the strength we need for every day's circumstances. No more, no less. Just enough.

My friend, don't be discouraged by your weaknesses. God knows your need—He really does. It's human to be tired after a mom's full day, but how we handle our tiredness is of the utmost importance. Our power for living must depend on faith in the source of our power—Jesus Christ.

· · · · ·

Lord, You are my strength. When I feel weak, let me rely on You. I will not let Satan take advantage of my tiredness. Instead I turn to You and receive the victory set aside for me in You. Amen.

Pruning Hurts

He cuts off every branch in me that bears no fruit,
while every branch that does bear fruit he prunes so
that it will be even more fruitful.

JOHN 15:2 NIV

My husband is a real believer in pruning all our trees and shrubs each year. I can't stand to go outside on those days. For years I've said something like, "Bob, you are killing the plants. They will never grow back." And for the same number of years, Bob has replied, "Emilie, you wait and see. In a few weeks the plants will be more beautiful than before." And you know what? Every year the plants have come back more beautiful than ever!

Throughout Palestine, vines grow abundantly, and every year gardeners prune the branches so the vines will produce high-quality fruit. Branches are considered useless unless they produce. Fruitless vines are drastically cut back, and the pruned limbs are destroyed. The Old Testament pictures Israel as the vineyard of God, so the vine became a symbol for the people of God. Jesus called Himself the true vine, using the vine and branches as an analogy to show how a believer must abide in Him.

Jesus' followers are the branches on God's vine. The branches have no source of life within themselves, but they

51

receive life from the vine, from Jesus. Without the vine, the branches produce no fruit. Perhaps at times you feel like a shrub being pruned. You want to cry out, "Stop! I've had enough!" When you do that, are you hearing God say, "I'm answering your prayers"? The unnecessary, the unproductive, must be cut off from your life so that the fruit will appear. Pruning is necessary in nature, and it is necessary in your life as My child. Remember, I am the one doing the pruning. Pruning is a painful process, but it does not last forever. One day your cut branches will sprout forth new growth and fruit will appear."

* * * * *

Father God, let me listen to You when You are pruning my life. Help me not to yell "stop," but instead, to look at the shears and know that You have my best in mind. I look forward to bearing new fruit for You. Amen.

Makeover of the Heart

People look at the outward appearance,
but the LORD looks at the heart.
1 SAMUEL 16:7 NIV

Reality TV shows are the latest fad. We've all seen them. Many of us have watched and wondered, "If I were on the show, how would they change my home?" or "How would they change me?" Shows that focus on personal appearance promise to transform featured people into the "perfect" human being. Some shows even focus on plastic surgery, and the participants choose "perfect" parts—nose, eyes, lips, breasts, thighs, and weight. The people can change their looks so drastically they wouldn't even recognize themselves!

As I leaned back on the sofa, I realized that altering my physical appearance would not change the real me. I reflected on today's Scripture in 1 Samuel. If beauty really is skin deep, then that leaves a vast possibility of loveliness existing and exuding from within a person. The question to ask is, "Am I beautiful in God's sight?" What needs the extreme makeover for most of us—the inside or the outside?

In deep conversation with a Pharisee named Nicodemus, a ruler of the Jews, Jesus explains the delicate transformation of the needed heart makeover. He said that an outward appearance of devotion was simply not enough (John 3).

In the conversation that follows, Nicodemus finally asks Jesus the all-important question: "How can someone be born when they are old?...Surely they cannot enter a second time into their mother's womb to be born!" (verse 4 NIV).

Jesus told this Pharisee that he must be born of the flesh *and* the Spirit. Now that is the ultimate extreme makeover.

You might be asking the same question in life. Inside your soul and heart you are yearning for a peace you aren't experiencing in your everyday life. You look into the mirror and your physical body looks okay, but there are unsatisfied tensions in your inner self. If you find yourself in the same situation as Nicodemus, Romans 10:9-10 explains how to get that extreme makeover:

> If you declare with your mouth, "Jesus is Lord," and believe in your heart that God raised him from the dead, you will be saved. For it is with your heart that you believe and are justified, and it is with your mouth that you profess your faith and are saved (NIV).

While we fret over our physical appearance and often waste time pondering what we would change if we had the chance, Jesus is right here offering the ultimate makeover—the one that truly will change our lives. He offers a makeover of the heart.

• • • • •

God, don't let me get caught up in the world's thought patterns that declare I need an extreme physical make-over. Let me be satisfied with how You created me. Help me concentrate on my inner qualities so that I will become more like Christ. Amen.

The Four "With Alls"

You shall love the Lord your God with all your heart, and with all your soul, and with all your mind, and with all your strength.

MARK 12:30

For decades our culture has encouraged each of us to "do our own thing." You know the mottos: "I know what's best for me," "Don't tell me what to do," and "If it feels good, do it." In the wake of those values, we've seen an increasing lack of accountability in each succeeding generation. In contrast, one noted Christian said, "The rule that governs me is this: Anything that dims my vision of Christ or my prayer life, or makes Christian work difficult, is wrong for me, and I must, as a Christian, turn away from it."

Which motto do you want to live by? The emphasis on "I" that the world values will be broadcast loud and clear throughout our lives. If we are going to learn anything different, if we are to live by godly values and be willing to assume responsibility for our actions, it's up to us to make it happen. We don't learn these things by accident or fall into them naturally.

Search your heart today and see if you are accepting responsibilities readily, admitting your mistakes easily, and serving God with all your being. How are you to love God?

- with all your heart
- with all your soul
- with all your mind
- with all your strength

* * * * *

God of love, give me the will and power to love You with the four "with alls." I want the passion to love You this way every day and forever. Amen.

You Can't Out Give God

One person gives freely, yet gains even more; another withholds unduly, but comes to poverty. A generous person will prosper; whoever refreshes others will be refreshed.
PROVERBS 11:24-25 NIV

I have found today's verses to be a basic principle in life: Giving pays tremendous dividends. Most of our riches are in friends, support groups, and those who give encouragement. As we have refreshed others, the Lord has refreshed us through these gifts.

One of our favorite mottos is "You can't out give God." Mark, in his Gospel, quotes Jesus saying that if we give up worldly possessions for Him, we shall receive a hundred times as much in the present age—homes, brothers, sisters, mothers, children, and fields (Mark 10:29-30). Wow! What a return of blessings for those who serve the Lord.

I'm so thankful for all God has given to me. He has abundantly bestowed so much on me and my family. Take time today to think of all the blessings in your life—and then give God your thanks and praise.

* * * * *

Father God, the principle of giving You have shared with me is amazing. My life is so much richer because of what You teach me. Thank You. Amen.

God's Timetable

*There is a time for everything, and a season for
every activity under the heavens...[God] has made
everything beautiful in its time.*
ECCLESIASTES 3:1,11 NIV

One great accomplishment in life is learning to find rest
in our appointed time—relishing the joys and challenges that come with each new stage of living. These include
the excitement and possibilities of youth, the satisfaction and
fulfillment of maturity, and the wisdom and patience of later
years. As we advance in age, though we see our youth and its
aspirations fly by, we gather wonderful memories to cherish
and discover new lessons to learn. We anticipate more and
more eagerly the time of being with the Lord for eternity.

I have learned that God has a master plan for my life,
and I am comforted in knowing I live by His timetable. I
have already experienced so many seasons—each one good
in its own way. Why shouldn't I expect the next stage to be
good as well?

God is the potter and I am the clay. He will mold me and
make me in His special way. I encourage you to remain pliable and flexible so God can mold you more easily, forming
a perfect vessel for the life He has planned for you.

* * * * *

Father, You are my friend. I know You will work all things together for my good. Help me be more flexible so I will more readily follow Your plan for my life. Amen.

A Record Mile Run

I can do all things through [Christ] who strengthens me.
PHILIPPIANS 4:13

One evening my grandson Chad, who was in the sixth grade at the time, called and wanted to know which verse of Scripture said that a person could do all things. After thinking for a few moments, today's verse came to mind. I asked Chad why he needed to know. He replied that the next day he was running the mile for the Presidential Physical Fitness Certificate, and he was really nervous about it. He said his stomach was churning, and he wasn't going to be able to sleep, which would cause him to be tired tomorrow. He was worried he wouldn't do well. He wanted to read this verse so he could be at ease and do a good job in the race.

We talked for a while. I had a word of prayer with him and then hung up the phone. The next morning I called to see how he'd slept, and he assured me he was good and rested. He also said his mom had prepared a high-energy breakfast for him. He was off to school with confidence that he could do his very best.

That afternoon, around three-thirty, the phone rang. Chad was on the other end. With a cheerful voice he stated, "Grammy, I won the race in record time! I know that the verse and your prayers really helped me. I will always remember that verse when I need reassurance. Thanks, Grammy."

What a thrill to realize that a 12-year-old boy went to Scripture to get help. Is that our first thought? To go to God and His Word when we are worried, anxious, and even hopeful? We too can learn to run a better race when we seek the leading and strength of the Lord.

. . . . .

Lord, I do know I can do all things through You. You are my strength and my assurance. You help me when things are tough. I love You! Amen.

Keep Your Word

A faithful man will abound with blessings.
PROVERBS 28:20

We are repeatedly challenged to understand what it means to be faithful to God. We know we're supposed to be dedicated and committed, but when we see faithfulness wavering in the lives of those around us, it can be difficult to remember what it means to have this virtue. The first thing we must do is look at our actions. When we exhibit the fruit of faithfulness, we show up on time, do what we need to do, and finish the job. One of our family's favorite mottoes is "Just do what you say you are going to do." Can you imagine what a difference living this out would make on the job, with your spouse and children, at church, and in every area of your life? The results would be amazing!

A successful life is based on trust and faith. Throughout the Old Testament, we read of God's faithfulness to the people of Israel. No matter how much the Israelites complained about their situation, God remained true to His chosen people. In the New Testament, Jesus reflected the same loyalty to His heavenly Father. He always sought God's will. Jesus' faithfulness took Him all the way to the cross so that our sins could be eternally covered.

Do you trust God and have faith in His leading as you journey through your own deserts, through your own trials? Do you stand for faith and follow through on what you say you are going to do? Some of us have had people cross our paths who have not kept their word to us, and it has hurt us deeply. That can make it difficult to trust people around us and even difficult to trust God. One of the best ways to overcome the fear of relying on God's strength alone is to become a strong and faithful servant. You will discover that as you keep your word and focus on being honorable and righteous, it is less important to you what others do and say. What truly matters is how faithfully you are following God's leading.

Scripture makes it very clear what it means to be faithful. Someday we will stand before God, and He will welcome us into heaven by saying, "Come in! Well done, good and faithful servant!"

• • • • •

Dear Lord, You have said that I am to be faithful. I want to be known as a faithful person who honors You. Amen.

Finding Complete Happiness

Enter His gates with thanksgiving and His courts with
praise. Give thanks to Him, bless His name.

PSALM 100:4

I had a very close friend who said, "If only I could have a bigger house, a bigger car, a bigger ring, live in a certain city—then I would be happy." Even though this satisfaction and craving for more often leads her down the path of depression, she continues to look for happiness in whatever she doesn't have. Do you find yourself echoing that longing for things? Do you have a secret or public list of items, accomplishments, or possessions you want before you'll be content?

The Scriptures are quite clear that a thankful heart is a happy heart. To have complete happiness we must enter into the Lord's presence with thanksgiving. I have found that when I am appreciative for all I have, my mental, physical, and spiritual dimensions are balanced with each other. The family chores run smoother, and the mood of my home is more relaxed. I'm excited to bounce out of bed each day, challenged by what may come my way. During this time of peace and tranquility, my friends seem to bond closer to me.

I'm fun to be around. There is an air of positivity transmitted from my presence.

People like to be around people who are upbeat and edifying. We build up instead of tear down. A smile and laughter are ever-present on our faces. We need to take our eyes off of stuff and become women of thanksgiving. When we are thankful, possessions are in proper perspective and happiness will not elude us.

• • • • •

Father God, take away my focus on acquiring things. Let me be a person with a thankful heart. I know my happiness does not depend on acquiring possessions. Help me break away from materialism. I thank You for all I have. Amen.

Be Willing to Say "Thank You!"

*Love is patient, love is kind and is not jealous;
love does not brag and is not arrogant.*

1 Corinthians 13:4

As believers, we must be sensitive to the fact that we don't want to take our spouses for granted. After more than five decades of marriage, my Bob and I continue to work on this area of our life together. We do little courtesies for each other all the time. He is such a gracious gentleman wherever we go. Women often comment to me what a warm, soft, and tenderhearted man he is. He still opens my car door and lets me enter buildings first. He brings me flowers and takes me to special shows. He asks rather than tells me, considers me equal to him, and willingly seeks and listens to my opinions. He is always ready to say thank you.

Likewise, I'm continually extending my appreciation. I never want to be void of my thankfulness for my Bob as my husband.

Taking a mate for granted is one of the main reasons our country experiences more than a 50-percent divorce rate. And second and third marriages have an even higher percentage of failure. Please don't get caught in the trap of expecting your mate to do things just because he is your spouse. Everyone needs appreciation and encouragement.

As the years fly by, Bob and I continually discuss our feelings toward each other. Are we still filling each other's "emotional tanks"? Are we drifting into complacency?

Appreciation is a choice. Choose today to stop taking your spouse for granted. Get excited about life and its many challenges. Choose to be grateful—and then express your appreciation. The more you do, the easier it becomes. You will have a fuller and richer life when you focus on thankfulness.

* * * * *

Lord, don't let me become complacent about my mate. I want to always be an encourager. Thank You for giving me a husband who affirms me as a woman. He plays a large part in helping me develop into the woman You want me to be. Amen.

Help Wanted

A cord of three strands is not quickly torn apart.
ECCLESIASTES 4:12

Many times we look to others to help us out, and we complain when we don't receive the help we think we deserve. However, help starts from within ourselves first, and then it comes from outside.

As a busy mom, I usually had to depend on me to get something done. Often there was no one around to help during the hectic schedule of a busy day. Perhaps your life is like that too. Take heart! You will get everything done that needs to be done. At such times, it helps to take an inventory of all the skills and tools God has so graciously given us at birth. We tend to take for granted these attributes for success that were given at the very beginning of our lives. What am I talking about? Our eight fingers and two thumbs.

Although we need to dig in and do our own work, sometimes we do need the help of others. King Solomon in all his wisdom tells us that friends are great blessings to us:

- Two are better than one because they have a good return for their labor (Ecclesiastes 4:9).
- Woe to the one who falls when there is not another to lift him up (verse 10).
- If two lie down together they keep warm (verse 11).

- If one can overpower him who is alone, two can resist him (verse 12).

- A cord of three strands is not quickly torn apart (verse 12).

Are you working on relationships that build these friendly blessings? Begin at home with your family members. Throughout Scripture we are reminded to be united, to be of the same spirit, to be of one accord. Unity should be our goal: wife to husband, parents to children, children to siblings, friend to friend. Your church is a great place to reach out too. How well do you know the other mothers in your church? Have you offered help to another mom when she needed it? A good family church is a great place to build a network of moms who can help each other through the rough times of raising children.

· · · · ·

Lord, let me fully realize the gift of my hands. May I also be more appreciative of the friends You have given me. Remind me to be available to serve other people, especially other mothers. Amen.

Redemption of Time

I will make up to you for the years that the swarming locust has eaten... You will have plenty to eat and be satisfied and praise the name of the LORD your God.
JOEL 2:25-26

In the history of farming, growers have had their crops decimated by the invasion of swarming locusts. Farmers have had to move hundreds of miles and, on occasion, even find new lines of work because the locusts destroyed their way of life.

But our God is a God of restoration! Even when the devastation to a human being is like the work of a swarm of locusts on a promising crop—even then God promises to completely restore everything that has been destroyed.

Have the locusts eaten anything of yours? Your health, a job, a reputation, a husband, a friend? We all have had losses due to locusts in our lives. Perhaps you have already experienced God's restoration and are rejoicing. But you may still be looking out over the fields that were once full and rich with bounty but are now destroyed. Look up! Your fields can be restored. The Savior's promise for Israel can also be claimed for your life. Yes, you can even praise God for the locusts of the past. Their devastation was simply a pathway for God to move. And when God moves to restore, He does an awesome job.

God renews our past by renewing our present. He gives us new peace, new joy, new goals, new dreams, and new love. What God has promised, He will do!

*   *   *   *   *

Lord and Healer, please restore my emptiness to fullness, my brokenness to wholeness, and my weakness to strength. You are a mighty and gracious God! I am so grateful for the way You sustain me today and forever. Amen.

Inspiration for Your Quiet Moments

❧ ❧ ❧

Quiet In-between Times

Quiet moments on-the-go might be the only way you can experience them. If you are in and out of the car on some days, transporting your loved ones to their activities or your own, think about creating a quiet-time basket. A picnic-sized basket or a single-handled bread serving basket will do for this visual reminder to seek stillness during your day. Pack a journal, Bible, book of prayers, and anything else that helps you savor moments alone with God.

During the week, take note of welcoming spaces that are near your frequent stops. These are spots you could use for your personal time: a lovely neighborhood park near where you wait for your child during sports team practice, a churchyard with inviting benches, a river walk area with stretches of grass in the sun and shade, even a cute café with an outdoor table. These can become your sacred spaces.

Let Your Child Be Your Teacher

Behold, children are a gift of the LORD,
the fruit of the womb is a reward.
PSALM 127:3

We so often think we are to be our children's teachers, but in reality they can also be our teachers. As our children respond to us in verbal and nonverbal fashion, they often are not very kind with their rebuttals. Often as we walk away from a meeting with our children (no matter what ages they are), we feel less confident and more vulnerable than we did before the encounter. My children taught me much about patience, how to handle confrontation, unconditional love, respect, problem solving, rejection, and the ever-changing aspects of life.

Amid your child-rearing frustrations, take on the attitude that your children are teaching you some very valuable facets of character development. Rather than becoming upset with their uncooperative behavior, ask God, "What are You trying to teach me in this situation?" Take these opportunities to discover important insights into life. When you look at your children as teachers, you won't become nearly as irritated by their behaviors and responses.

As your children notice how you respond to them, they will be more willing to improve their communication with you. They have observed that you are a better listener, and that you aren't as reactionary as you had been.

Try this strategy the next time you feel yourself becoming defensive after one of your children's remarks. Ask, "What can I learn from this situation?" God may be talking to you through your child.

. . . . .

Father God, help me be willing to learn from every situation I encounter. I know You can use my children to teach me. I look forward to learning whatever You want me to know. Amen.

How to Love the Rich Life

The love of money is a root of all sorts of evil, and some
by longing for it have wandered away from the faith
and pierced themselves with many griefs.

1 TIMOTHY 6:10

One of our young grandchildren asked Papa Bob, "Are you rich?"

"Yes—in the Lord," he answered.

"No, Papa. I mean really rich," he insisted.

He wanted to know if his grandpa was monetarily rich. You know, the good old capitalist word "money."

Regardless of where most of us are on the financial barometer of life, we are rich compared to someone—especially when we consider the world's population. Just by living in America we are rich. Many of us have blessings and abundance that we look past because we are so focused on what we don't have and what we want.

We need to examine our attitude toward material wealth. And the result of that examination should determine how we live. Do you know that how we live communicates what our concept of wealth is to our children and others? A simple lifestyle demonstrates that whatever riches we have aren't the most important priority in our lives. Let's be good stewards of the gifts God has given us by giving generously of our time and financial resources to people in need. And include your children in discussions about how and where to give to others, so they learn the value and pleasure of giving.

Exhibit that your security and peace don't come from your bank account, but from your relationship with Christ. Live in such a way that your children and others will understand that the riches in heaven are far more exciting and enduring than riches on earth. Teach them that it really is more blessed to give than to receive.

* * * * *

God, You are a provider of abundance. I want my family members to be worthy stewards of all You choose to bless us with. Help us evaluate our spending and lifestyle from Your perspective. Thank You for the riches You give to us. Amen.

Growing Daily in Godliness

*The lazy man longs for many things,
but his hands refuse to work.
He is greedy to get, while
the godly love to give!*
PROVERBS 21:25-26 TLB

I believe a godly woman possesses inner peace and tranquility. She doesn't have to prove herself to anyone. She is strong, and yet she doesn't use her strength to control or dominate people. Neither does she depend on recognition from others. Hers is an inner contentment and satisfaction based not on accomplishments, position, or authority, but on a deep awareness of God's eternal and personal love for her.

That kind of peace, strength, and confidence comes from depending on God, obeying Him, drawing on His strength and wisdom, and learning to be like Him. When this happens, we gradually grow free of anxious competitiveness and aggressiveness. We have no need to prove our value because we know how much we are worth in God's sight. That makes us free to reach out in love to others.

I've seen this spirit at work in the lives of so many beautiful Christian women—women of all ages and in every walk of life. I think of a young lady who was 25 years old when I first met her at the Edmonton airport in Alberta, Canada. In the two days we spent together, I could see the spirit of godliness shining in her life. She had a vision for her family and the women of her church to become more Christ-centered, and that vision was contagious.

I also think of a lovely 92-year-old woman who attended one of my organizational seminars. This amazing lady sat through all four sessions, scribbling notes the entire time. I remember thinking, "At 92 who even cares?" But this new friend told me she wanted to learn everything she could in life so she could pass on her knowledge to younger women. Her teachable spirit humbled and blessed me. I only hope that when I am 92 I will be as eager to learn and grow in God's grace.

Godly values—spiritual awareness, obedience, trust, self-giving love—are so different from the values that run this worldly age. And yet God's strategy for growth and happiness has been around for more than 2000 years. Countless generations of women have found that it works. I pray that we will take it seriously as well, growing daily in godliness and modeling godliness in our homes and lives.

* * * * *

God, I need a daily reminder regarding what my true priorities are in life. Help me be more Christlike every day. Amen.

Be a Sower of Seeds

*I am the vine; you are the branches. If you remain in
me and I in you, you will bear much fruit;
apart from me you can do nothing.*

JOHN 15:5 NIV

smart woman once told me that a wise person does in her youth what a fool does in her old age. Let's not wait until we are old to do what we should have done when we were young. Here are two well-known and biblical principles: Whatever we sow, we will reap. The harvest always comes *after* the planting. All other things being equal, we can anticipate that with good weather and adequate rain, we will have a large crop—if we have made the effort to sow in the first place. In a sense, I am experiencing a harvest time in my life right now. I am reaping the results of friendship seeds sown in other seasons.

I remember busy times when I almost didn't have time for friends—when a phone call, or a note, or a luncheon date, or even a word of prayer was truly a sacrifice of my time. Making time for others was truly a struggle. How glad I am that I made those efforts to sow seeds of friendship and love and to cultivate those crops carefully. Now I have the privilege of reaping an abundant harvest. I am so blessed to have my family, friends, and loved ones around me. Through their expressions of love and kindness, they share Christ with me.

* * * * *

Loving Father, help me today to keep my heart and mind focused on You, Your goodness, and Your blessings in my life. Thank You for giving me such loving family members and friends. Amen.

Deep Roots

*Blessed is the one who trusts in the LORD, whose con-
fidence is in him. They will be like a tree planted by
the water that sends out its roots by the stream.
It does not fear when heat comes; its leaves are
always green. It has no worries in a year of
drought and never fails to bear fruit.*

JEREMIAH 17:7-8 NIV

So many women share with me, "I'm just dying for a
little peace and quiet—a chance to relax and think
and pray. Somehow I just can't seem to find that in my life."
"Stillness" and "silence" are not words many of us even use
anymore, let alone experience. We all desperately need the
chance to grow deep roots that will provide nourishment,
strength, and stability for us during the hard times. My journey through cancer brought much hardship, but it also provided many hours of waiting, listening, and sitting in silence.
I was forced to slow down and grow roots.

Almost every day for five years I had to lie down for a
nap. These were precious times of restoration, and I wouldn't
trade them for anything. Too bad that it took an illness to
teach me to clear my calendar to find these precious times
of quietness.

I encourage you to do whatever is necessary to nurture
the spirit of silence in your life. Don't let the enemy wear

you down and steal your balance and perspective. Regular time for silence is as important and necessary as sleep, exercise, and nutritious food. The door to silence and stillness is waiting for any of us to open and go through, but it won't open by itself.

* * * * *

Father God, help me choose to be still. Give me the courage to turn off all the noise in my life so I can spend time alone with You. Amen.

Good News Before Bad

All Scripture is inspired by God and profitable for teaching, for reproof, for correction, for training in righteousness; so that the man of God may be adequate, equipped for every good work.

2 TIMOTHY 3:16-17

Some days I wake up and reach for the morning paper or turn on the TV to catch the latest news. After all, it's important to be well informed about world events. But after a few short days of this, I'm reminded of a saying I once heard: "Read the Good News before you read the bad news." And that's absolutely right. Why would any woman carrying so many family responsibilities want to start the day off with the bad news from the headlines before she reads the Good News in Scripture?

When I start off my day by reading and reflecting on God's Word, I am energized. I handle my responsibilities, choices, and emotions with God's wisdom leading the way. As I look back over the years, I know that the times when I skipped my morning moments with the Lord were also the times when I encountered frustration and experienced a lack of focus. I seemed to move along from one small crisis to the next without peace or purpose.

Even if logic tells you that you have no time or energy to set aside for *anything*, trust your heart and turn to the Good News each morning. It will enrich your life with goodness.

· · · · ·

Father God, I pray for the energy and discipline it will take to commit to time with You each day. It is what I long for. Please gently urge my spirit to enter Your presence. I want to draw from the source of the Good News before I face the busy day. Grow my passion for this daily activity, Lord. Amen.

Home Robbers

The worries of the world, and the deceitfulness of riches,
and the desires for other things enter in and choke the
word, and it becomes unfruitful.

MARK 4:19

If we're not on guard, the things of the world will enter into our homes and rob us of contentment. We get trapped in "I need this," "I don't have enough of that," "if only my kitchen were bigger," "my dishes are so old," "I don't have the right wallpaper," "the cupboards need a fresh coat of paint," "I can't entertain until I have new carpet," and so on. Do these joy-robbing phrases sound familiar? Have you uttered a few of them?

I encourage you to take a moment to be refreshed. Instead of focusing on a home beautiful, contemplate a home filled with the spirit of loveliness—the spirit of warmth and caring. I've talked with thousands of women like you who truly have a heart for home. Your situation may be unusual, but like most women, you probably want to be a home builder not a home robber.

Do you long for a home that is warm and welcoming, comfortable and freeing? A place where you can express the uniqueness of your God-given talents and nurture your relationships with people you love? Do you desire a home that reflects your personality and renews your soul? A place that glows with a spirit of loveliness? I believe this spirit is already in your heart. You can stop the home robbers at the curb and not give them access to your home.

No matter how little or how much you have, you can experience the results of having a godly home. Take steps toward making your home a sanctuary—a place of security, trust, and comfort. A place to reenergize, pray, and dream. You can begin with a friendly welcome at the front door for your family and friends.

Father God, there are so many people who want to steal the joy of my home. Cast away those acquaintances who are negative in thought. I want to cherish my family and friends who build up my desire to reflect Your spirit of loveliness in my home. Amen.

Being Passed Over

*Not from the east, nor from the west, nor from the desert comes exaltation; but God is the Judge;
He puts down one and exalts another.*

PSALM 75:6-7

Nothing hurts like being passed over in life when you feel like you should have been selected for the team, chosen for the lead in the play, elected president of the club, or perhaps loved by that handsome football player you had a crush on in high school. Today's verse is for all of us who have been left out. We all have wanted a certain position and didn't get it. We all have felt the sting of rejection, and there's perhaps only one thing more painful—watching our children be passed over for something they've set their heart on.

At such times, we are the ones to whom they turn for consolation. You'll be called on to offer a lesson in how to have a stiff upper lip in times of disappointment. The wise mother will point her disappointed child to today's powerful verses from the book of Psalms.

God will lift up in His time, not ours. This is a hard, but very valuable life lesson. God knows our hearts, and He is *always* wise in His decisions. Perhaps it is someone else's time right now, and it will help your child heal if he or she learns to rejoice with those who are rejoicing. Remind your children that their day will come, and it will be even sweeter for them because they will know God chose the time for them to be picked.

And Mom, live your life as an example. Your family will witness your patience and your faith in the One who heals all wounds, including those caused by rejection and disappointment.

. . . . .

Father God, take from me the desire for earthly recognition. Let me focus on the task, not on the reward. I know that You will lift me up in Your time. I trust You for that. Help me be a supportive mom when the time comes for me to comfort my child when he or she has been passed over. Amen.

Asking "Why?"

God is our refuge and strength, a very present help in trouble. Therefore we will not fear, though the earth should change and though the mountains slip into the heart of the sea; though its waters roar and foam, though the mountains quake at its swelling pride.

PSALM 46:1-2

When disaster strikes in a faraway land, when someone we know faces serious illness, when we are left heartbroken after a great loss, we can feel like our faith is shaken to its core. Have you ever shouted out to God, asking where He was in the time of your need? Have you cried with deep grief and questioned how God could let something so bad happen?

It seems very human to ask this "why" question at such times. Our inquiring minds want to know. Why would a loving God permit destruction, devastation, and death? The sad fact is, we live in a fallen world, and events happen according to the laws of nature. Because of the sin of mankind, there will always be things that happen other than what we would choose in a perfect world. There will be troubles and suffering beyond our control. At such times, our comfort comes from God's Word. In today's verses we find three comforts in such events of life:

- God is our refuge.
- God is our strength.
- God is always ready to help in times of trouble.

If we can internalize these "big three" promises we can live with this victory:

- We will not live in fear.

What great assurance we can have even when our souls quake. We can apply these promises to every event of life—tsunamis, earthquakes, heartbreaks, and soul quakes. Just remember, when we walk through life's storms we have two choices:

- respond as a faith-filled person
- respond as a faithless person

A faith-filled person will respond in these ways:

- She delights in reading and knowing God's Word.
- She meditates on God's law day and night.
- She's like a tree firmly planted by streams of water.
- She yields fruit in its season.
- Her leaves don't wither.
- She prospers in all things.

This woman of faith understands where she comes from and where she is going. She is not one who questions God because of the events of the world. She doesn't look to the world for the answers of life. She is firmly grounded in what God assures her, even when the quakes occur.

· · · · ·

Dear Lord, help me stand on Your promises when the hardships of life come my way, as they surely will. Give me the faith to trust Your Word. Amen.

When Faith Seems Lost

*Wives, fit in with your husbands' plans; for then
if they refuse to listen when you talk to them
about the Lord, they will be won by your respectful,
pure behavior. Your godly lives will speak to them
better than any words.*

1 PETER 3:1 TLB

ob and I were hosting a radio talk show in Southern California when a lady called in and asked, "How do you love a husband who isn't a Christian?" I thought for a moment and then replied, "The same way you would love a husband who is a Christian."

Too often husbands who aren't believers—and even some who are—feel they are in competition with Jesus for the love of their wives. That is definitely not how to love your husband, whatever his faith. These men often give up on their marriage relationships because they believe they can't compete for their wives' devotion against someone as good as Jesus. Wives do indeed need to love God with all their hearts, souls, and minds (Matthew 22:37), but they are also to love their husbands—even when their husbands have hardened their hearts or strayed from the Lord.

Standing by your man when his heart is hard against God is difficult, but it may be easier if you understand a few things first:

- Realize that you are not responsible for your husband's salvation.
- You are not appointed to be the change agent in his life.
- Your husband's salvation is between God and him.

Are you relieved to discover that your husband's salvation isn't your responsibility? I meet so many women who take on this responsibility and then feel like failures time after time. Often they turn those feelings of failure into worry and even anger toward their husbands. And that, in turn, causes them to stop offering and showing godly, loving behaviors to their spouses, and it makes their marriages miserable.

So ultimately what is your role if your husband's heart isn't open to the Lord? Your role is to love him. Today's Scripture verse gives very clear direction on what you are to do. Let those words encourage you to stand by your man. But also recognize that fitting in with his plans won't always be easy.

. . . . .

Father God, give me the courage to step out in faith based on Your Word. Let me be willing to trust and obey. When I need it, remind me that You are in charge of my husband's relationship with You. Amen.

Don't Forsake Me

Now that I am old and gray, don't forsake me.
Give me time to tell this new generation
(and their children too)
about all your mighty miracles.
PSALM 71:18 TLB

There is a season of life that challenges our belief in the hereafter. What happens when we die? The psalmist pleads for God not to forsake him until he declares the power of God to the next generation. Wow! What a great prayer! I guess that's why I do what I do. I want to tell everyone, starting with my immediate family and branching out to others, about the power and might of God.

One of my favorite passages of Scripture gives me a vision of how I can touch the next generation. It's found in Titus 2:3-5 NIV:

> Likewise, teach the older women to be reverent in the way they live, not to be slanderers or addicted to much wine, but to teach what is good. Then they can urge the younger women to love their husbands and children, to be self-controlled and pure, to be busy at home, to be kind, and to be subject to their husbands, so that no one will malign the word of God.

If only we could grasp the vastness of these words. Don't wait until you are old and gray haired. Begin today!

· · · · ·

God, I need You. Take control of my life. Make me the kind of person You want me to be. Amen.

The Strength to Change

If anyone is in Christ, the new creation has come:
The old has gone, the new is here!

2 CORINTHIANS 5:17 NIV

*T*hey say you can't teach an old dog to change, but I want to tell you that you can. In fact, if you do something for 21 consecutive days, you will usually create a new habit. We as believers in Christ must realize that we no longer want to be as we were. That since knowing Jesus, we have become people of hope and love. We no longer like who we used to be. Becoming a woman of God begins with making a personal commitment to Jesus Christ. Only He can give us the fresh start that allows the Holy Spirit to abide in us and grow strong.

Today's verse reminds us that we are new creatures in Christ. That's what I discovered many years ago when I, a 16-year-old Jewish girl, received Christ into my heart. My life began to change from that moment on, and the years since then have been an exciting adventure with Jesus Christ!

It hasn't always been easy. I've had to give up much bitterness, anger, fear, hatred, and resentment. Many times I've had to back up and start over, asking God to take control of my life and show me His way to live. But as I've learned to follow Him, He has guided me through times of pain and joy, struggle and growth. And how rewarding it has been to see spiritual maturity take root and grow! I give thanks and praise for all God's goodness to me over the years.

And I'm not finished yet! Far from it. Growing in godliness is a lifelong process. Although God is the One who makes it possible, He requires my cooperation. If I want to be more Christlike and to have Him shine in my life and in my home, I must be willing to change what He wants me to change and learn what He wants to teach me.

· · · · ·

Lord, I realize that change is possible. Give me the strength to change so I will become more like You. Amen.

Joy Comes in the Morning

Weeping may go on all night, but
in the morning there is joy.
PSALM 30:5 TLB

It's okay to cry, so don't try to hide it. Be real if you're going through a struggle. Your illness, trial, or loss is real. The people around you need to know that you feel the pain deeply. That's one of the blessings of a difficulty that is too great to hide—it forces you to be vulnerable with the people around you. Struggles take away the phoniness of life, and you gain a new understanding of how precious each new day of being real with yourself and others is. The things you used to think were important aren't nearly as important now. Life is viewed with a new perspective.

Do you know what the other blessing is? The more real you are with others, the more genuine they will be in their responses to you and your trial. If you've spent years keeping people at a safe distance because you were afraid to reveal your weaknesses or your worries, trust God to shape those relationships into more meaningful connections. You will learn how freeing and life changing it can be to embrace the joy of honesty. Be open during your conversations with dear friends and family members. Children, depending on their ages, don't always need to know everything; however, they need to be aware that life is difficult for you at the moment. This knowledge gives them an opportunity to learn compassion.

Even amid the sorrow, each new day holds and reflects the joy of Jesus. His promises and His love will be made more real to you.

· · · · ·

Father God, help me be brave even when tears flow. Let me know that it's okay to cry. Please give me joy in the morning. Amen.

A Great Return

*May he multiply you a thousand times more
and bless you as he promised.*

DEUTERONOMY 1:11 TLB

To know that my blessings will be increased a thousand times is almost beyond comprehension. After all, a bank might give me 3 percent interest on my savings, but a 1000-time markup is simply unbelievable. Yet this is exactly what I am promised in today's Scripture. The Lord has promised to increase my blessings—and your blessings—a thousand-fold. Wow!

Of course, this verse is talking about more than money or possessions. It's also talking about a return on investment in family, emotional stability, marriage, health, desires, and all other components of life. And it doesn't have a time limit, either. Perhaps some of the blessing I'm promised will happen in eternity and in the lives of those who come after me on this earth.

Still, I know that God keeps His promises. And what a promise this is! Knowing my blessings are growing and growing and growing gives me strength—even amid the uncertainties of this life.

* * * * *

Father God, sometimes I am discouraged by the day-to-day grind of life. Calm me today. Help me set my sights on things above and give You thanks. Amen.

Inspiration for Your Quiet Moments

❧ ❧ ❧

Scents for Stillness

A fresh scent that triggers memories of a spring afternoon or a holiday gathering will bring with it a sense of delight and calm. Use scents throughout your home or have a sachet near your special place for quiet time.

The simple ingredients you use for potpourri can become the base for fragranced items throughout your home. Your potpourri mixture, crushed and stuffed into little muslin or calico bags, can serve as sachets in drawers and closets. For an extra-pretty sachet, make little lace hearts lined with tulle or netting and fill with potpourri or wrap a little potpourri in a lace handkerchief and tie with a narrow ribbon.

Be a Woman of Serenity

Cast all your anxiety on him because he cares for you.
1 PETER 5:7 NIV

The dictionary defines "serene" as "calm, clear, unruffled, peaceful, placid, tranquil, and unperturbed." Do these words describe any place or anyone you know? Maybe the Grand Canyon? Maybe a wise woman who has discovered the peace of our Lord and learned how to rest in Him? That dictionary definition of "serene" describes so few places and people in today's world. We have fast-food restaurants, drive-through lines, cell phones, second-day mail, next-day mail, fax machines, tablets, smart phones at work, at home, and even in the car.

We yearn for peace and quiet, but where do we turn? We must turn to God. We have to become quiet *inside* so His still small voice resonates through our every cell and reverberates in our hearts and souls.

We need to be quiet before the Lord to fully experience His peace and His restoring touch. We need to listen to what He teaches us and hear where He would have us go. We will benefit greatly from such times with our heavenly Father and experience peaceful calm.

A woman who is serene settles the environment just by her presence. She is at peace with those around her. A serene woman is sensitive to nature and aware of all aspects of her womanhood. She is willing to help make the world better. She is not so rushed that she can't give her husband and family her time. Her home will reflect this serenity, encouraging people to relax. Guests will ask, "How do you ever leave this house? It is so comfortable! I feel such tranquility when I'm with you, and it's so good to relax." Has anyone told you this lately?

One key to finding serenity is learning to let life happen around you. You don't have to be involved in everything. Sometimes it is very right to say no to requests. Let go of those things you can't control. Serenity and tranquility are gifts from God. They come when we trust Him as our Lord, Shepherd, Guide, and Protector.

* * * * *

Lord, I want to slow down and become more serene in my life. Place me around women who will hold me accountable to this desire. Amen.

How Is Your Heart?

O God, my heart is quiet and confident.
No wonder I can sing your praises!
PSALM 57:7 TLB

A quiet and confident heart sounds so lovely, doesn't it? This kind of heart gives us stability in a life that's constantly saying, "Faster, faster! Hurry, hurry!" Few of us have this kind of heart. One of our common pleas is "How do I find the time?" One way to get started is to make morning devotion time a priority for your life. Put it on your daily planner (the same as any appointment), and have your spouse hold you accountable for this commitment. Morning is a great time to meet God because it gives you a great start for the day. Some of us are morning people and some are late-evening people. You decide when the best time for you to meet with the Lord is.

Psalm 5:3 gives us motivation to meet God: "In the morning, O LORD, You will hear my voice; in the morning I will order my prayer to You and eagerly watch." What kind of structure might you have? Here are some suggestions:

1. Pray for guidance so that you focus and dedicate this time just for God and you. Begin by praising God for who He is (Psalm 148:1-5).

2. Read a portion of Scripture. If you are new to the faith, you might want to start in the book of John (Psalm 119:18).

3. Have a time for prayer. You might want to use the word "ACTS" to remember four areas to include:

> **A**—Adoration. This segment is all about God. You love Him, you adore Him, you thank Him for all He's done for you. Reflect on who He is (read Lamentations 3:22-23).

> **C**—Confession. You agree with God on what sins you have committed and ask for forgiveness. He will grant it! You will leave your time with God with a clean heart (read Psalm 66:18).

> **T**—Thanksgiving. Be specific in thanking God for all He has given you. Thank Him for your marriage, your family, your home, your pastor, your job, and so on. Even thank Him for your difficult times—after all, these are events that create growth in your life (read 1 Thessalonians 5:18).

> **S**—Supplication. Make your requests known to God. Remember to include requests for others, such as government officials, missionaries, students, believers in other countries (read Matthew 7:7-8).

Become a member of the morning watch. There are no membership forms to fill out or monthly dues. It takes 21 days to start a new habit. Begin today and see how it will have a positive influence on the rest of the day—and transform your life.

* * * * *

Father God, I want to meet You first thing for the morning watch. When the alarm goes off, help me jump out of bed enthusiastically and be on time for our appointment. Amen.

Take Time to Rest

Come to Me, all who are weary and
heavy-laden, and I will give you rest.
MATTHEW 11:28

f you've ever gone to the Grand Canyon in Arizona, you have seen those burden-bearing mules that carry goods, people, and materials down to the canyon floor. They seem so small yet they carry such heavy loads. As you look at their swaybacks, it doesn't seem like they can continue one more step.

Jesus saw people that way—as burdened and stressed, weighed down by the legalism and legalistic demands the Pharisees had placed on them. No matter where they turned, some politician was telling them what to do or what not to do. Matthew 23:4 states:

> They tie up heavy burdens and lay them on men's shoulders, but they themselves are unwilling to move them with so much as a finger.

We don't need religion that becomes an unbearable burden. We need rest from the terrible burdens that sin and hopelessness create. That's why Jesus came! He came to give rest by lifting the weight of sin from our shoulders. God opened the way for full and free living just as He originally intended for us to experience. To walk in obedience to God is never a burden—it's freedom.

It's also physically healthy to rest from the stresses of life. In order to live long, we must reduce the pressures in our lives. Prioritizing will help us cast off the hurry of today's technological age. Never in the history of mankind have we been under more pressure to perform. We are molded into thinking we must have a perfect marriage, a perfect family, a perfect career, a perfect home. Because of this pressure, we will break if we don't relax. Jesus says to come to Him and He will give us rest!

• • • • •

Father God, I don't know what life would be like if You weren't alongside me to ease my burden. You have given me such great relief. Thank You! Amen.

Becoming One

So we, who are many, are one body in Christ,
and individually members one of another.
ROMANS 12:5

In Scripture we often hear the terms "one spirit," "one belief," "one life," and "one another." That's when we begin to realize that God wants us to grow in "oneness." Togetherness in the body of Christ helps bond our relationship with God. Early in the book of Genesis we read, "For this reason a man shall leave his father and his mother, and be joined to his wife; and they shall become one flesh" (2:24). Ephesians 4:12 NIV says,

> Christ himself gave the apostles, the prophets, the evangelists, the pastors and teachers, to equip his people for works of service, so that the body of Christ may be built up until we all reach unity in the faith and in the knowledge of the Son of God and become mature, attaining to the whole measure of the fullness of Christ.

When we join forces with others, we become stronger and it becomes difficult to weaken our positions. There is great strength in unity. This concept is at the center of why we need to be in a church that's teaching God's Word every time we meet. We need the support of others if we are to

111

grow in Christ. Today I want you to examine various Scriptures to impress upon you the importance of oneness:

- ❧ Romans 12:5 regarding belonging to one another: "We, who are many, are one body in Christ, and individually members one of another."

- ❧ Romans 12:10 regarding being devoted to one another and honoring each other: "Be devoted to one another in brotherly love; give preference to one another in honor; not lagging behind in diligence, fervent in spirit, serving the Lord; rejoicing in hope, persevering in tribulation, devoted to prayer, contributing to the needs of the saints, practicing hospitality."

- ❧ Romans 12:18 regarding living in harmony with one another: "If possible, so far as it depends on you, be at peace with all men."

• • • • •

Father God, help me realize how important it is to have a support system of fellow believers who have kindred spirits. I can't walk this life journey alone. I need friends who will encourage me and lift me up in You. I am not an island. Amen.

Use What You've Been Given Wisely

To everyone who has, more shall be given, and he will have an abundance; but from the one who does not have, even what he does have shall be taken away.

MATTHEW 25:29

God has given each of us specific talents—to some more than others, but to each of us something. What kind of stewards are we to be with these talents? Some of us know from personal experience how a stuttering child can become an eloquent speaker or, conversely, how a brilliant debater can become homeless when his talent is wasted or misused.

Today's verse is from a passage where Jesus tells His disciples that the kingdom of heaven is like a man who called his servants together. He delegated to each of them a portion of his property. To one servant he gave five gold coins, to another two coins, and to the third one coin. Each servant was given according to his ability.

The first man traded with his five coins and doubled his master's money. The man with two coins did likewise. But the man with one coin dug a hole in the ground and buried it.

After a while the owner of the land came to settle the accounts with his three servants. The first servant brought with him the original five coins plus five additional ones. The master said, "Well done, good and faithful slave. You were faithful with a few things, I will put you in charge of many things; enter into the joy of your master" (Matthew 25:21).

The second man, who had been given just two coins, brought forth the original two plus the two he had made. The master likewise said, "Well done, good and faithful slave. You were faithful with a few things, I will put you in charge of many things; enter into the joy of your master" (verse 23).

The third servant came forward with the one gold coin and said, "Master, I knew you to be a hard man, reaping where you did not sow and gathering where you scattered no seed. And I was afraid, and went away and hid your talent in the ground. See, you have what is yours" (verses 24-25).

But the master replied, "You wicked, lazy slave, you knew that I reap where I did not sow and gather where I scattered no seed. Then you ought to have put my money in the bank, and on my arrival I would have received my money back with interest. Therefore take away the talent from him and give it to the one who has the ten talents" (verses 26-28).

Then Jesus stated, "To everyone who has, more shall be given, and he will have an abundance; but from the one who does not have, even what he does have shall be taken away" (verse 29).

The third man didn't mean any harm to his master, but he didn't understand the principles of stewardship and faithfulness. When we are faithful, we are reliable: appearing on time, doing what we say we are going to do, being present when we need to be, going beyond what is expected, and finishing the job we started.

Throughout Scripture, God reveals His faithfulness. And we too are to operate on that principle. Everyday life operates on the laws of faith and trust. We assume people are going to honor their word, stop at red lights, pay monthly mortgage or rent, pay the utility bills, show up for appointments, and be faithful in marriage.

We want to be women who will reach out with one or two or five talents and invest them wisely in our homes, marriages, churches, families, and communities. We want to be women who will take what we have and double it so that when we stand before Jesus He will say, "Well done, good and faithful servant! Enter into the joy of my Father's mansions." What a glorious day that will be!

· · · · ·

All-knowing God, I live in a world that makes comparisons. I look around and often see people who have five talents, while You seem to have neglected me by giving me only one. I wonder, "How can I be as good as that person since she has so much more than I do?" I pray that You will clearly show me how I can be faithful with the talent You have given me. Thank You, Lord, for all You provide and for loving me enough to guide me in how to use it. Amen.

Is It Mud or Beauty?

Whatever is true, whatever is honorable, whatever is right, whatever is pure, whatever is lovely, whatever is of good repute, if there is any excellence and if anything worthy of praise, dwell on these things.

PHILIPPIANS 4:8

One Sunday morning we were going to the airport in Maui, Hawaii, and it began to rain. We were surprised when the shuttle bus driver said excitedly, "This is a day for celebration!" When she noticed our expressions of curiosity, she explained that in Hawaii, if rain falls on your wedding it will bring good luck. We looked at each other and both agreed that in Southern California, if it rained on your wedding it would be a disaster. Strange how people look at things differently.

On one rainy day, a woman overheard another person say, "What miserable weather!" The woman looked out of her apartment window to see a big, fat robin using a nearby puddle of water for a bathtub. It was having a wonderful time splashing water everywhere. The observer thought, "Miserable for whom?"

Another example of diverse perspective was when a young boy watched an artist paint a picture of a river. The boy told the artist he didn't like the picture because there was too much mud in it. The artist admitted there was mud, but what he saw was the beautiful colors and contrasts of the light against the dark.

There are different ways to view the same scene, the same moment, and the same circumstance. Mud or beauty—which do you look for as you travel through life? Do you tend to see the mud—and a great deal of it—as you look at the day ahead or even as you review the past? Is it possible that there are gentle hues and surprising colors blended in as well? Take another look at the day, the moment, or the memory and discover where there is beauty.

As the apostle Paul taught in today's verse, we are to look for and think about things that are true, honest, right, pure, lovely, of good repute, and things with excellence. Look for the best and see the beautiful in everything each day. We have often heard the expression, "What you see is what you get." That's exactly what life is all about. Look beyond the mud and see the beautiful contrasts between the light and the dark. This is the way to get the best and most out of life.

The next time you are moaning and groaning because you want something beautiful, shiny, bright, and lovely in your life, take a moment in prayer and then observe how God has already placed something truly beautiful in your life—even in the midst of a rainy season.

* * * * *

Father God, help me look at life with a perspective focused on seeing Your beauty in my surroundings. Amen.

Give Us This Day

Our Father who is in heaven, hallowed be Your name.
Your kingdom come. Your will be done, on earth as it
is in heaven. Give us this day our daily bread. And
forgive us our debts, as we also have forgiven our
debtors. And do not lead us into temptation, but
deliver us from evil. [For Yours is the kingdom and the
power and the glory forever. Amen.]
MATTHEW 6:9-13 (brackets in original)

The "Lord's Prayer" is a model for our prayers. It begins with adoration of God, acknowledges the sovereignty of God's will, asks provision of Him, and ends with an offering of praise. The fatherhood of God toward His children is the basis for Jesus' frequent teaching about prayer. "Your Father knows what you need," Jesus told His disciples, "before you ask him" (Matthew 6:8). Jesus presents a pattern that the church has followed throughout the centuries.

Prayer begins by honoring the name of God. He is worthy of honor because He is the heavenly King who rules over everything. Because He is our loving King, we can entrust all our physical needs to His provision, asking Him to give us our food for today, instead of worrying about the future.

Since God is our merciful Father, we also seek forgiveness from Him while we extend His forgiveness to those who have sinned against us. Finally, we ask our Father to keep us from yielding to temptation and to deliver us from the evil one, for our God is able to defeat any evil that comes against us.

This model of prayer should be engraved on our hearts—and the hearts of our children. Information stored in our memory banks can't be taken from us and is available during our times of need!

* * * * *

Lord Jesus, Your model prayer has come to me in the night on several occasions and given me great comfort. Your prayer has become my prayer, and I enjoy reciting it often. Amen.

And It Was Good

And God saw that it was good.
GENESIS 1:18

As women on the go, we often don't take the time to see, hear, and smell God's creation. We find ourselves being so busy that we don't take the precious time to study God's creation in its fullness. Do you see evidence of God when you look around you? As I'm writing, the day is foggy where I live, and I can spy a single drop of dew on a leaf just beyond my kitchen window. With the sun breaking through the fog bank, this little drop of moisture is giving back to God a tiny sparkle of light that He sent from heaven.

Shakespeare spoke of "a gentle dew from heaven." He too must have taken a pause to look at a droplet of God's creation. He too must have been moved by the wonder of even such a small sample of God's work. I can fully understand how God looked at His creation—the earth and sky and waters—and confirmed that it was good. In fact, it's glorious!

When you work at something and create something, do you take a moment to call it good? We get so busy and so focused on productivity and moving on to the next thing on the list that we forget to take that moment and honor God by offering up that creation to Him. Just like that little drop of dew, our efforts can reflect God's light back to heaven.

It isn't prideful to be satisfied with your work. When you put your all into something, whether it is cooking a meal for your family, coordinating a volunteer work party at your church, painting a room, or completing a work project that took a lot of research and diligence, it is important to take a moment and praise God, celebrate, and simply take a moment to rest before you start something new. Slow down and wait until the Lord tells you, "It is good."

* * * * *

God, it is so good to know You created the droplets left by fog. It's so good to know You care about even the smallest elements of my life. Amen.

House Hunting

My Father's house has many rooms; if that were not so,
would I have told you that I am going there to prepare
a place for you? And if I go and prepare a place for you,
I will come back and take you to be with me that you
also may be where I am.

JOHN 14:2-3 NIV

There are different passages a couple travels through life. I clearly recall when my Bob and I realized we had to sell the "Barnes' Barn" after 16 years and move back to Newport Beach, California. It was a very tearful experience to leave our home after all those years, but we needed to move so I could get the best medical care after contracting cancer. It was time to move on.

Looking for that new, perfect home was another adventure. Bob and I were each drawn to different houses. Our Realtors, bless their patience, kept showing us homes on the market. Then one day our sales rep called and said she had the perfect house to show us. It met all the qualifications on our wish list. Sure enough, it was just what we were looking for!

How thankful we are that, as Christians, we do not have this problem regarding our heavenly home. Jesus assures us that He has already located, purchased, and closed escrow on our mansion in heaven. He promises to take us there to be with our Father forever. What a comfort to know that when believing loved ones die they have moved into that perfect home made just for them. No "For Sale" signs on the lawn! They are ushered into their heavenly home to spend eternity with our Lord.

·　·　·　·　·

Lord Jesus, thank You for assuring us that You have gone before us and paid the price for our eternal salvation. We look forward to being with You in heaven. Amen.

My Hiding Place

I love Your law. You are my
hiding place and my shield.
PSALM 119:113-14

As a little girl, I loved to play hide-and-seek. After the sun had gone down and it started to get dark, I delighted in finding a secret place where no one could find me. When I stayed there, I felt so secure knowing no one was going to catch me. As I grew older, I kept looking for such a place where I could get away from the pressures of life. When I became a Christian and started to have daily quiet times with my Lord, I was soon aware that my "prayer closet" had become my new hiding place. This was a place where I felt safe from the world. It was a place I could take all the time I needed to read God's Word.

My "prayer closet" is an actual place in my home, but I can transport the security of my sanctuary to the beach, to a mountain cabin, or to a desert condo. My place of prayer is wherever I meet with God. You too can create the same refuge no matter where you live. Don't confine your quiet time to just one location. God's comfort and love is our hiding place whenever we need it.

Do you talk to God throughout the day? If not, how come? Do you think your life isn't important enough or your concerns aren't big enough? Or do you just get so busy that it doesn't occur to you to talk to God while you're in the car, at work, or waiting for the kids to get out of school? Don't miss out on the wonders of communication with God. Being able to run to His embrace in every moment is one of the many gifts we receive as believers. He is right there with you.

When the stress of the day is getting to you, think of the safety you feel in your hiding place. Knowing God is always with you will calm your spirit.

. . . . .

Father God, I look so forward to meeting You each day at our appointed time. Your Scriptures still my soul. And I know I can meet with You anytime for any length of time—even just a few seconds on a busy freeway. My anxieties are washed away after our time together. Thank You! Amen.

Loving One Another

*Two are better than one because they have a good
return for their labor. For if either of them falls, the
one will lift up his companion. But woe to the one who
falls when there is not another to lift him up.*

ECCLESIASTES 4:9-10

*Y*ou would think that after more than 50 years of marriage, my Bob and I would have it all together. Everything figured out. Everything wired. Everything humming along like a well-oiled machine. That's a nice thought, but marriage is not a machine. It's a human relationship, and every relationship needs work, care, and attention—and sometimes suffers from neglect and withers a bit through indifference.

To this day Bob and I put daily thought, effort, and prayer into our relationship. Are there still speed bumps along our marriage highway? Of course there are. And those are times when we need to humble ourselves before God and each other to make things right. And Bob and I not only live together as husband and wife, but we also work together. Many women have told me it would be a disaster for them to work with their husbands; that it would be way too stressful and frustrating. Yet Bob and I have worked together in business and ministry for more than 30 years! Though we'll never be perfect, we've established a way of working in harmony and love toward goals we value and desire.

Bob's strengths compensate for my weaknesses, and my strengths compensate for his weaknesses. We balance one another and help each other in those areas where each of us needs the most assistance. Isn't that what Solomon was talking about in today's verses from the book of Ecclesiastes? Bob and I understand one another's temperaments, we know each other's quirks, and we're aware of each other's uniqueness.

Here is my most important message from this devotion:

> Let your man know you need him.

"Well, Emilie," you say, "I think he already knows that."

Are you sure? It's like that old cliché about the man who never says "I love you" to his wife. "Why should I?" he grouses. "I told her I loved her on our wedding day 49 years ago, and if that ever changes, I'll let her know." That wouldn't cut it with you, would it? Why? Because you want to hear those crucial words. You want him to look you in the eyes and speak those words to you from his heart as often as possible. And when he does, it fulfills something deep inside you.

When my Bob tells me he loves me, it feels like everything is right in my world—no matter what else is going on. Admittedly, I've had to work with him on this communication through the years. I've told him, "Honey, if you tell me you love me every day, I'll be a happy woman the rest of my life."

And it's really no different for a man. He also needs to hear you say "I love you." And he also needs to hear you say you need him. Being needed is a vital part of a man's makeup.

* * * * *

Gracious God, please help me take nothing for granted in my relationship with my husband. Show me how to be an encourager for him at all times. Amen.

More Than Words

I am convinced that nothing can ever separate us
from [God's] love. Death can't, and life can't.
The angels won't, and all the powers of hell itself
cannot keep God's love away.
ROMANS 8:38 TLB

Words, words, words! Sometimes that's what the Bible seems to me. Sometimes it seems confusing or hard to understand. Sometimes—especially when life was going well—I would read through entire passages without any sense of what the words really meant. But during the tough times, the times when my life began to crumble, I found that the words of Scripture really came to life. Passages I had previously read and memorized leaped to my mind and helped me cope with my situation. The Word suddenly took on new depths of meaning.

The familiar words of Romans 8:38 are a wonderful comfort. They remind me that the Lord is with me in my pain, and that He also is greater than my current situation. He is larger than my pain, larger than any fear I may have, and larger even than death. I have often needed that assurance and been unsure of my own strength.

Nothing can separate me from God's love—and that's more than just words! That's rock-solid, dependable, life-giving truth. Praise the Lord!

· · · · ·

Lord God Almighty, You are perfect in power and love. Amen.

Pursue Peace

Peace I leave with you; My peace I give to you.
JOHN 14:27

The world likes peace. They like the idea of it, and they like to talk about it. Peace symbols adorn buses, backpacks, and bumper stickers. Peace is pleaded for everywhere and in every language. Lasting peace is certainly what we need, and isn't it true that it is also what we crave? However, most people are looking for it in the world or through the world's offerings. And they often equate happiness or the fulfillment of their desires as peace. But peace defined by the fruit of the Spirit is an assured quietness of the soul. It is the opposite of our earthly struggles and is best described as a "wellness between oneself and God." It isn't about reaching career goals or having life easy. It is about a healthy relationship with our Creator.

The peace that God gives is built on the awareness that we all have purpose and cause for existing. As we mature in our spiritual nature and learn what this life is all about, we discover that only our heavenly Father can give us lasting calmness within. Once we realize this, we no longer toss and turn, trying to find answers to our daily struggles. We have reconciled with God through Jesus, His Son, that life has meaning in Him, and we are created in God's image. We

131

know Jesus, the alpha and the omega. We finally know who we are. We have inner tranquility of mind, soul, and spirit. There is a calmness to our presence that is recognizable as God's peace.

When our lives reflect God's love and joy, those around us will be drawn to us and see the outward expression of this fruit of the Spirit. They'll want to know where they can get it—a perfect opportunity for us to share our Lord's love and provision.

• • • • •

Lord, may I continue to be willing and patient to develop my life toward the precious virtue of peace. Help me to always point people to You as the source of ultimate peace. Amen.

Inspiration for Your Quiet Moments

🌸 🌸 🌸

Put a Tingle in Your Toes

*A*hhh. When you treat your feet right, your entire body relaxes. Here is an easy way to refresh your spirit and take joy in a simple pleasure.

Boil 8 cups of water and then add 1 tablespoon table salt and five sprigs of fresh or ten sprigs of dried peppermint. Let stand until water is warm and comfortable. Pour into a bowl and soak your feet for 10 to 20 minutes. Rinse with cold water and apply lotion.

This is a wonderful way to settle into bedtime or just a time of relaxation!

Approaching God's Throne

Our Father in heaven, hallowed be your name.
MATTHEW 6:9 NIV

*L*et's spend more time in the beauty and peace of the Lord's Prayer. It is one of the most precious prayers of the Christian faith. And it all begins with this adoration of God: "Our Father in heaven." God tenderly invites us to know that He is truly our Father, and we are truly His children so that we may ask of Him in all cheerfulness and confidence, as dear children ask of their dear father.

We all go through periods when we act more like stubborn children than willing ones. We want to do things ourselves our way because we like the control. And we think that puts us in charge. Of course, it really doesn't. Such behavior puts us further away from God's direction and will for us. Life actually becomes more out of control, chaotic even. And we never have the peace that comes from resting in our Father's wisdom and truth.

James 4:2 states, "You do not have because you do not ask God" (NIV). We try many ways to cope with the stresses of life. Often we escape into work, leisure time, body toning, and exercise, and even many kinds of addictions. These escapes look like viable ways to survive, but behaviors turned to as responses to stress—even those with religious trappings—are not the solution. God wants us to boldly approach His throne and commit our requests, our adoration, our thanks, and our supplications to Him in the form of prayer.

God is the *only* one who can direct us to live life as He meant it to be. Since God is so near to us, we can approach Him in a very personal way. When we open our prayer with the phrase "Our Father," we acknowledge that the answers of life lie beyond our abilities, our looks, our social position, our economic status, and our work. We admit that our might is not enough to live the fullest life that God intended for us. We have to be very brave to admit we need someone bigger than we are. But we can call on the Father in confidence, knowing we are His children and that He loves us and hears us.

We gain strength and confidence when we call on God by name and admit that we need Him for our every need, that we are helpless without Him.

. . . . .

My Father in heaven, thank You for allowing me to come to Your throne. I need You today and every day. I am so privileged to be Your child. You show me how to love, how to forgive, and how to rest in Your peace. Thank You. Amen.

Today Is a Gift

We were under great pressure, far beyond our ability to endure, so that we despaired of life itself.

2 CORINTHIANS 1:8 NIV

Does today's verse sound like your life? Well, maybe not quite as despairing, I hope. But your complex role as a woman, especially a busy mom, is almost beyond description. Without doubt you have one of the most difficult, demanding, and taxing job descriptions in the world. When I'm out shopping, I see moms with little children, and I quickly think back to the days when I had the same responsibilities.

For all of us, whether we are parents or not, the ever-increasing pressures and stresses of living are sometimes intense, making it impossible for us to live the abundant life we all seek. Dad is pressured on the job. Profit margins are getting smaller, and competition is getting more fierce. While striving for excellence at work, Dad also wants to be a loving husband, father, and leader of his family. Maybe you face the same stresses of being in the workforce. What big responsibilities we carry at different times in our lives.

What stresses do you face regarding the management of your household—keeping the children focused, satisfying your husband, and maintaining a proper balance in your life?

As Christians, we can endure these stresses successfully if we view life's pressures as opportunities for us to demonstrate God's power. How we respond to our various pressures helps shape us into the people we will be tomorrow. If it takes all these stresses to make us into the women God designed us to be, then all these uncomfortable situations will make the trials worthwhile. These efforts, challenges, and blessings of responsibility are God's means of revealing His strength as we tackle the duties we face daily.

Yesterday is history, tomorrow is a mystery, today is God's gift. That's why we call today "the present." Look on today as a gift from God to you. No matter what pressures the day brings—it truly is a treasure. With each inconvenience you meet, may you realize that this too is merely a building block to becoming the person God designed you to be.

· · · · ·

Father, no one enjoys the pressures of life. Help me look at them as teaching tools sent by You to help me become the person You want me to be. Amen.

The Lost Mitt

*The Lord will continually guide you, and satisfy
your desire in scorched places, and give strength
to your bones; and you will be like...a spring of
water whose waters do not fail.*

ISAIAH 58:11

It was my son Brad's first real leather baseball mitt. Bob
taught him how to break it in with special oil to form
the pocket just right for catching the ball. The oil was rubbed
into the pocket. Then Brad tossed his baseball from hand
to hand to form a pocket just right for him. Brad loved his
mitt and worked for hours each day to make it fit just right.
He was so happy to have such a special glove for his games
and practices.

One afternoon after practice, one of the older boys asked
to see Brad's mitt. He looked it over and then tossed it into
a grassy field. Brad ran to find his special possession, but he
couldn't find it. Nowhere was his mitt to be found. With a
frightened, hurt heart, Brad came home in tears.

I encouraged him by saying that the mitt was there some-
place and we'd go look.

"But, Mom, I did search the lot, and it's not there,"
replied Brad in tears.

So I said, "Brad, let's pray and ask God to help us." By
now it was beginning to get dark, and we needed to hurry,

so we jumped into the car. As I drove to the baseball field, we asked God to please guide our steps to the exact spot where the glove was. After parking, we quickly headed into the field. Again we asked God to point us in the right direction. Brad ran into the tall grass. He went about 20 feet and found his glove.

God answers our prayers! Sometimes it's "wait," "yes," or "later." For Brad, that day it was a yes. God said in essence, "I'll direct you, My young child whose heart was broken because of a bully, to your lost glove."

Do you have a "lost glove" today? Go before God and praise Him for the promise He gives in today's verse. If God says it, believe it! He will direct you and guide you. Open your heart to listen to what His directions are and then press ahead. The grass may seem too tall for you to see very far, but trust the Lord and keep walking until you feel in your heart the peace you desire. God may lead in a direction you least expect, but step forward with confidence in Him.

• • • • •

Lord, what an encouragement to me that You care about the smallest details of my life. I want to be a spring of water to those around me. Amen.

Share Your Cup

God has given each of you some special abilities;
be sure to use them to help each other, passing on
to others God's many kinds of blessings.

1 PETER 4:10 TLB

When the Lord fills our cup, He intends us to pour it out. He encourages us to fill the cups of others with His love. And when we do, the sweetness of His love and peace flows from cup to cup. I would never have guessed when I was a young wife many years ago that one day I would write books and conduct seminars to help women get organized, care for their homes, love and care for their families, and live as women of God. You see, I had only a high school education and didn't feel adequate to tell anyone what to do.

How did all this begin? Little by little, women recognized my gifts for organization and speaking. They affirmed my worthiness and encouraged me. Some invited me to share what I knew with their women's groups. Over the years, as I made use of my gifts to administer God's grace to others, I've felt His grace overflow in my own life as well.

Don't let this time in your life go unchallenged by change. Even in seasons of despair, reach up and grab on to helping others with the gifts God has given to you.

· · · · ·

Giver of all gifts, my prayer is that each woman I meet will discover and use the gifts You have given her to help someone along the way. And help me use my gifts to point people to You. Amen.

If I Could Do It Again

*There is an appointed time for everything. And there is
a time for every event under heaven.*

ECCLESIASTES 3:1

Repeating something from the past so that you can do it better, more perfectly, or more lovingly is a nice thought, but none of us are granted do-overs in this life. We can wish all we want, but we can't do life again. As deeply as I might like to go back to certain seasons of my life or revisit certain attitudes or decisions I made in my younger years, I can't do it. No one can. God has placed each one of our lives on a timeline, with a specific beginning and a specific end. And wherever we may be on that line, going forward is our only option.

We've looked at the next verse before, but let's revisit it. One good thing about studying the Bible is that we can go back to verses over and over. And our lives will be better off for such returns! This verse is encouraging and comforting, especially when we are tempted to revisit the past or spend long stretches of time dwelling on our mistakes:

> "I know the plans I have for you," says the Lord. "They are plans for good and not for evil, to give you a future and a hope" (Jeremiah 29:11 TLB).

We can't go back, and we can't stand still. We can move forward in the plans God has for us. We can know that we have the peace and security of God's love and His grace. In that peace we can rest in hope and in what's to come.

We have to take life as it comes. Each day brings a fresh opportunity to follow the Lord and—in His power and grace—begin life anew from this point forward. Praise His name! The Lord's mercies "are new every morning" (Lamentations 3:23). So yesterday is yesterday and today is today, and life must be lived with faith and in God's great abundance, joy, and purpose in the 24 hours directly before us.

No matter how much we trust the Lord, no matter how deeply we dip into His resources, there will always, always be more…infinitely more. We can't trust the Lord too much, and all of us trust Him way too little.

Even if you look back and wish you'd realized this more in your younger days, you can do something about it in your life now. As a woman, wife, and mother, place more of your trust and faith and confidence in God and His Word. I promise you'll never regret doing so.

· · · · ·

Father God, keep me from dwelling on what I should have done in the past. Instead, help me be excited by what I can do now and in the future with Your help. Amen.

Why Is God Worthy of Worship?

[God] has made everything beautiful in its time. He has also set eternity in the human heart; yet no one can fathom what God has done from beginning to end.

ECCLESIASTES 3:11 NIV

God has given us an eternal perspective so that we can look beyond the routines of life. Nevertheless, He has not revealed all of life's mysteries. When we're feeling down or going through difficult times, two major questions we ask are "Why is this happening?" and "Is God worthy of worship?" Mankind has been asking these basic questions throughout history. Is it because God works out every detail of our lives? Or because the good guys always win? Is it because God always answers our big and difficult questions about life?

If we went to the time of the book of Ecclesiastes and addressed this question to the "teacher," he would say that "God is worthy of worship simply because He is God." God doesn't promise only good things will happen to His followers. Even when life is filled with pain, heartache, and uncertainty, God still remains worthy of praise and worship. Even in hard times we must decide if we will "fear God and keep His commands" (Ecclesiastes 12:13). The writer of this great book of the Bible asserts that even though life sometimes seems meaningless it has its satisfactions:

- ❧ Knowing God puts things in perspective (Ecclesiastes 2:24-25).

- ❧ Satisfaction with our work is His gift to us (3:13).

- ❧ There is strength and comfort in human companionship (4:9-12).

- ❧ All our deeds are in God's hands (9:1).

Even with his great wisdom, the "teacher" (Solomon) could not figure out all the mysteries of life. Life has its unanswerable questions—and even some contradictions—but we face them knowing that Jesus has already overcome them, giving us hope.

Yes, God truly is worthy of our worship.

• • • • •

Father God, I know it's not very spiritual when I question Your greatness. Thank You for being so gracious and for reminding me that You are always present even when I feel alone. I stand confident that You will never leave me. Amen.

Isn't This the Carpenter?

Isn't this the carpenter? Isn't this Mary's son and the brother of James, Joseph, Judas and Simon? Aren't his sisters here with us?

MARK 6:3 NIV

Jesus wasn't accepted among the people of His hometown. They marveled at the crowds who gathered to hear the wisdom that came from His mouth. However, they were confused. "Isn't this the carpenter?" they asked. They thought they knew Jesus well. They couldn't believe that the man who grew up among them could be elevated to the prominence where crowds would gather to hear Him teach.

One man who proclaimed Christ is remembered even today although he took a vow of poverty and lived a very simple life. Saint Francis of Assisi died more than 775 years ago, but he has never been forgotten. Great men and women by the hundreds of thousands have lived and died—kings, conquerors, millionaires, artists, musicians, and scholars. All have been forgotten, but not Saint Francis of Assisi. The world stood back in wonder, for Saint Francis eschewed money but believed he was rich in Christ. This man's body was scarred and wracked with pain, yet he sang sweeter than any bird. He was a beggar who smiled as he dined with the famous and laughed as he shared his last crust with a leper.

He'd learned to love everything that lived as part of God's creation.

Saint Francis had a secret worth knowing, and the world has been learning it from him ever since. The secret is the wisdom of Jesus, whom some thought of as just a carpenter. This carpenter was a builder of lives. He used more than lumber to create His structures. He used plain, ordinary people just like you and me to further God's kingdom. Isn't that amazing?

As we are challenged to be like Jesus, may we, like Francis of Assisi, not let social status or societal limitations prevent us from becoming the person Christ wants us to be.

· · · · ·

Lord, I too can be more than ordinary. Light my path so I won't stumble along the way. Your light overcomes darkness and gives me hope for tomorrow. Help me share Your illumination with everyone around me. Amen.

Fear Not

When you go through deep waters and
great trouble, I will be with you.
ISAIAH 43:2 TLB

Do you know it's against God's character to give you a promise and not keep it? We live in a culture where many people make promises they don't keep. God is not like that. If He says it, He will do it. Don't let the world define for you what a promise is. If you do, you will be confused by God's Word. Remember, God cannot and will not break a promise.

Notice that in today's verse Isaiah says "when," not "if." Sooner or later, all of us will go through deep waters. If you aren't experiencing difficulties at the moment, you eventually will. Stand in line because your time will come.

When we are young or when life is treating us well, it's hard to think about the woes of life. "They might happen to others, but surely not to us or our families," we think. I vividly remember when my doctor announced to me and my family, "Emilie, you have cancer." I was devastated. I had read and heard about others who had cancer, but surely not me. I couldn't believe what I'd heard. Me? Surely not me! But it was true. If the Lord grants us an abundance of years, we will all experience woes. During that time of great woe in my life, I claimed God's promises:

- 🌱 God is with me.
- 🌱 The rivers aren't sweeping over me.
- 🌱 The fires aren't burning me.
- 🌱 God is calling me by name, and I will fear no evil.

Another passage of Scripture that I had read many times came alive to me. Not until I was walking in the valley of the shadow of death did I truly appreciate what was being taught.

> Consider it all joy, my brethren, when you encounter various trials, knowing that the testing of your faith produces endurance. And let endurance have its perfect result, so that you may be perfect and complete, lacking in nothing (James 1:2-4).

It has been many years since my doctor told me I had cancer. If anyone would have told me that I could or would be able to endure such a journey, I would have said, "No, I can't." However, God had a different lesson for me to learn when He declared, "Yes, you can!" Friends still ask me, "How did you do it?" My reply? "A day at a time and many days and hours at a time. And lots of prayer and great support from Bob, family, and friends."

If you find yourself going down a dark road, I echo Isaiah's words: "Take courage, fear not" (Isaiah 35:4).

* * * * *

Father God, You know I am not brave, but by Your grace and mercy You give me the strength to endure. Thank You. Amen.

Life Is More Than Abundance

*Beware, and be on your guard against every form of
greed; for not even when one has an abundance
does his life consist of his possessions.*

LUKE 12:15

One of our universal problems is the overcrowding of
our homes. Whether we have an apartment or a six-
bedroom home, it seems like every closet, cupboard, refrig-
erator, and garage are crammed with our abundance. Some
of us have so much that we even go out and rent additional
storage sheds and spaces for our possessions.

Bob and I are no different. We buy new clothes and cram
them into our wardrobes. A new antique goes in the corner,
a new quilt hangs over the bed, a new potted plant gathers
sunlight by the window. On and on it goes. Pretty soon we
feel as though we are closed in with no room to breathe. We
continually struggle to keep a balance in our attitudes regarding possessions.

Abundance seems like it would be very simple to manage
if you are single and live alone. It's just you adding to stuff.
Life becomes more complicated with a spouse and children.
You soon get that "bunched in" feeling. This creates more
stress, and you can lose your cool and blow relationships
when your calm is broken.

151

We made a rule in our home about abundance. Simply stated it says, "One comes in, and one goes out." After every purchase we give away or sell a like item. We used to have annual garage sales to clear the clutter too. When I buy a new blouse, out goes an older one. The same goes for a new table and so on. Naturally, if you're just starting out or are a newly wed this rule won't apply to you—yet—because you probably don't have an abundance of possessions.

There's another strategy that's also very effective. We've informed our loved ones that we don't want any more gifts that take up space or that have to be dusted. We prefer receiving consumable items.

Remember, life is not based on possessions. Share with others what you aren't using.

· · · · ·

Faithful God, help me incorporate this new principle in my life. I don't want to be stressed out because I own too much. Let me learn to be a giver and not a keeper of possessions. I need help in this area of my life. Amen.

Come Quick!

Don't hide from me, for I am in deep trouble. Quick!
Come and save me. Come, Lord, and rescue me.
PSALM 69:17-18 TLB

We want God to work everything out right now. Not tomorrow, but now—and hurry up about it. When life falls apart, we want it to be put back together right away. We don't want to struggle or see what comes after loss or after a big change has hit our circumstances, families, or hearts. We want to be rescued—right now!

And here is the good news…the God news: God will rescue us—but in His time, not at our usually desired hurried pace. This means that we may grow a lot in the area of patience and understanding. Yes, it takes work and rest and placing our hope in the Lord.

I certainly appreciate God's loving patience with me. I want to be known as a person of *being*—not just *doing*. I often ask God to keep me humble. Well, He has done that through my personal and long journey through cancer. I appreciate what God has done in my life. He has put a strong desire in my soul to spend time every day with Him. I ask Him, "Let time stand still, and let me forget all about my schedule during my time with You." I want to keep my focus on Him.

Don't overlook the days, months, or even years of grace and healing that follow any life trial. You will discover that God is with you, putting together the pieces with tenderness, mercy, and remarkable love. Your cries are heard by your Creator, and your tears never go unnoticed. Rest in Him today, my friend.

· · · · ·

Dear loving Father, please help me slow down and appreciate everything You give me. Heal my wounds—physical and spiritual. Help me reach out to others who are also struggling. Amen.

Fear of the Lord

The fear of the LORD is the beginning of wisdom;
a good understanding have all those who do His
commandments; His praise endures forever.

PSALM 111:10

The motto of the wisdom teachers in the Old Testament is that the fear of the Lord (showing holy respect and reverence for God and shunning evil) is the starting point and essence of wisdom. When we have a fear of the Lord, we express that respect by submitting to His will:

- Behold, the fear of the LORD, that is wisdom; and to depart from evil is understanding (Job 28:28).

- The fear of the LORD is the beginning of wisdom, and the knowledge of the Holy One is understanding (Proverbs 9:10).

- The fear of the LORD is the instruction for wisdom, and before honor comes humility (15:33).

Wisdom is not acquired by a mechanical formula. Instead, it's achieved through a right relationship with God. Doesn't it follow that obeying and living by God's principles and commandments should be the obvious conclusion to our thankfulness for all He has done for us?

In today's church world, many people have lost the concept of fearing God. The soft side of Christianity has preached only the "love of God." We haven't balanced the scale by teaching the other side of His justice and judgment—fear, anger, wrath, obedience, and punishment. Just because some pastors don't teach it from their pulpits doesn't make it less a reality. As with involvement with drugs, alcohol, lust, and envy, we must respect the consequences of our actions or we will be destroyed by their side effects. Our benchmark on all these life destroyers is to have a proper respect for God. He isn't a Big Daddy upstairs who never asks us to do anything we don't want to do. We must understand that there are consequences for those behaviors we adopt that go against God's will.

The good news is that when we are obedient to God's precepts, He helps us stay away from temptation. When we respect God, we commit our thoughts to Him and we choose to give our lives to Him. We desire His purposes for us. God will light the way for our paths, but we must be willing to follow His light.

· · · · ·

Amazing God, fill me with awesome respect for You. I want to be obedient to Your mighty precepts and principles. Amen.

You Don't Always Have to Win

*The anger of man does not achieve
the righteousness of God.*
JAMES 1:20

I don't know about you, but I've never won an argument. Even though my Bob might say, "I give, you win!" my heart feels heavy, certainly not victorious. It doesn't feel like we've been drawn together. In fact, disagreements drive us further apart. When disagreements arise, the interaction between the parties can be far from ideal.

An argument is when two or more parties are trying to prove their positions. Very seldom does anyone listen to learn anything. Each party is trying to overpower his or her opponent with oratory or volume. Rarely do people feel good in this situation; instead, there are usually feelings of resentment, anger, frustration, and stress.

However, if a person allows someone else to "win" a disagreement, it's often the case that both parties are winners. It's often a very rewarding experience that allows our relationship to grow. When you let someone else win, you are showing that it's no big deal to always be right. I know this can be a difficult assignment because in our competitive society we are taught that winning is everything.

When you are willing to let someone else win, you will find yourself better able to listen because you aren't trying to overpower the other person with the art of persuasion.

Yes, there are some critical positions that must be defended, but those are usually few in life. These points must be defended because of your moral and biblical position. Here are several key verses dealing with anger that will help us understand the disagreement process:

- A quick-tempered man acts foolishly (Proverbs 14:17).

- A gentle answer turns away wrath, but a harsh word stirs up anger (15:1).

- Do not let the sun go down on your anger (Ephesians 4:26).

- Everyone must be quick to hear, slow to speak and slow to anger (James 1:19).

* * * * *

Dear God, I appreciate that You have given me the ability to let someone else win an argument. Remind me that it's okay to not always be proven right. I know that letting someone else win doesn't mean I'm less a person because I also benefit. Give me Your wisdom for knowing when to stay the course and when to graciously give in. Amen.

Inspiration for Your Quiet Moments

❦ ❦ ❦

Create a Prayer Garden

A prayer garden is a special place where you can retreat and be alone with God. It's a place that helps you hear His still small voice, a place where the two of you can meet heart to heart.

Do you have a sunny spot in the yard? A sweetly shaded bench near some roses? Find a place in nature that can become your plot of prayer land. Place a bench and table there so you can take a cup of tea, a journal, and some notecards (to write friends telling them you prayed for them).

A prayer garden is a setting where your soul and your spirit are renewed and refreshed by spending time with the Lord.

Be a Light Wherever You Are

*You are the light of the world. A city set
on a hill cannot be hidden.*

MATTHEW 5:14

The parlor was tiny, just an extra room behind the store. But the tablecloth was spotless, the candles were glowing, the flowers were bright, and the tea was fragrant. Most of all, the smile was genuine and welcoming whenever my mother invited people to "come on back for a cup of tea." How often I heard her say those words when I was growing up. And how little I realized the mark they would make on me.

There were hard years after my father died. Mama and I shared three rooms behind our little dress shop in Long Beach, California. Mama waited on the customers, did alterations, and worked on the books until late at night. I kept house—planning and shopping for meals, cooking, cleaning, doing laundry—while going to school. After school I learned the dress business as well.

Sometimes I felt like Cinderella—work, work, work. And the little girl in me longed for a Prince Charming to carry me away to his castle. There I would preside over a grand and immaculate household, waited on hand and foot by attentive servants. I would wear gorgeous dresses and entertain kings and queens who marveled at my beauty and wisdom and brought me lavish gifts.

But in the meantime, I had work to do. And although I didn't know it, I was already receiving a gift more precious than any dream castle ever could be. For unlike Cinderella, I lived with a loving mother who understood the true meaning of sharing and joy. My mama brightened people's lives with her wonderful ability to make people feel comfortable when they were around her.

Our customers quickly learned that Mama offered a sympathetic ear as well as elegant clothes and impeccable service. Often they ended up sharing their hurts and problems with her And then, inevitably, would come the invitation, "Let me make you a cup of tea." She would usher her guests back to our living room/kitchen. Quickly a fresh cloth was slipped on the table, a candle lit, fresh flowers set out, and the teapot heated. If we had them, she would pull out cookies or a loaf of banana bread. There was never anything fancy, but the gift of her caring warmed many a heart on cold afternoons.

And Mama didn't limit her hospitality to just guests. On many a rainy day I came home from school to a hot baked potato fresh from the oven. Even with her heavy workload, Mama would take the time to make this little Cinderella feel like a queen.

My mama's willingness to open her life to others—to share her home, her food, and her love—was truly a royal gift. She passed it along to me, and I have the privilege of passing it on to others. What a joy to carry on her gift of entertaining friends and strangers.

• • • • •

Father, thank You for giving me people who loved and cared for me while I was growing up. Open my heart and give me a spirit of hospitality so I can readily share Your love with others. Amen.

Put on the New

*Choose life, so that you and your children may live
and that you may love the LORD your God,
listen to his voice, and hold fast to him.*

DEUTERONOMY 30:19 NIV

Life is a strange journey, but believe it or not, it isn't as complicated as many of us think. We have two options to choose from—either life or death. It's that basic. Not too much mental power is needed to figure this formula out. When we choose life, we love the Lord and we pay attention to His voice and direction. "If anyone is in Christ, he is a new creature; the old things passed away; behold, new things have come" (2 Corinthians 5:17).

What are these old things? They are the natural things that we are born with and the sinful things we need to flee from. These are things we need to put off:

- anger
- rage
- malicious behavior
- slander
- dirty language
- lying

You might ask, "What harm is there in keeping a few of those?" When you choose to keep any one of these, in essence you are choosing death. We must come clean and realize that these activities will eventually pull us away from God. He has a plan that spells out life. His perfect will for our lives is that we run as fast as we can from these "death" items. It means that once we're saved, once we've dedicated our lives to Christ, we will choose new friends, tell different jokes, read different magazines, hold our tongue when we want to scream in anger. No more gossiping or using foul language. These are all death knells to relationships, particularly in marriage and family life. So what do we want to put on? What does our new life look like?

> You are living a brand new kind of life that is continually learning more and more of what is right, and trying constantly to be more and more like Christ who created this new life within you. In this new life one's nationality or race or education or social position is unimportant; such things mean nothing. Whether a person has Christ is what matters, and he is equally available to all.
>
> Since you have been chosen by God who has given you this new kind of life, and because of his deep love and concern for you, you should practice tenderhearted mercy and kindness to others. Don't worry about making a good impression on them, but be ready to suffer quietly and patiently. Be gentle and

ready to forgive; never hold grudges. Remember, the Lord forgave you, so you must forgive others.

Most of all, let love guide your life, for then the whole church will stay together in perfect harmony. Let the peace of heart that comes from Christ be always present in your hearts and lives, for this is your responsibility and privilege as members of his body. And always be thankful (Colossians 3:10-14 TLB).

So what do we need to put on?

- ❧ mercy
- ❧ kindness
- ❧ humility
- ❧ gentleness
- ❧ patience
- ❧ forgiveness
- ❧ love
- ❧ thankfulness

We must be willing to take those things off that lead to death and put on those things that bring life.

*   *   *   *   *

Lord, give me the courage and strength to remove those things that will prevent me from being all You want me to be. I so want to be a woman after Your own heart. Help me to continue to dress in the things that bring life, especially love. Amen.

Becoming a Suitable Helpmate

The LORD God said, "It is not good for the man to be alone; I will make him a helper suitable for him."

GENESIS 2:18

Men love to be needed. They respond in a very positive fashion during those times when we ask for help. But most of us consider ourselves as very capable women and pride ourselves on our self-sufficiency and ability to get things done. And sometimes that leads us to believe we don't need help from anyone. Or at least that is the impression we give to those around us, including our husbands.

There is hope for us though. Many of us are beginning to realize that times of slowing down are important to our survival, sanity, and longevity. We understand now, after some years of trial and error, that the world's ideal of being a super-woman, a supermom, and a "superwife" is not God's ideal for our lives or our marriages. It is refreshing to ask for help and lean on our husbands' strength, wisdom, and help in our daily lives.

Just as we are called to be our husbands' helpmates, we are blessed to turn to them and say, "Honey, I need you. Will you please help me?" The simple, direct statement saying "I need your help" reinforces our husbands' value and place in our lives.

My question to married women is: "Are you a help or hindrance to your husband?" God created us to help our husbands in all they do. My observation as I read, study, and watch people is that American women have lost the focus of making their husbands their heroes. Scripture teaches the importance of having someone here to help us when we are in need. In Galatians 6:2, Paul calls believers to "bear one another's burdens, and thereby fulfill the law of Christ." Reaching out helps our needs get met and also creates a special bond with the person we let come near to give assistance. Sometimes being a helpmate means asking for help.

Take time to be an encourager to your spouse. Let him know you appreciate all he does for you and your family.

• • • • •

God, I truly want to be a helpmate for my husband. I want to fulfill the commission You have given to women from the time of creation. Guide me in Your direction. Amen.

You Can Touch Stars

*Forgetting what lies behind and reaching forward to
what lies ahead, I press on toward the goal for the prize
of the upward call of God in Christ Jesus.*

PHILIPPIANS 3:13-14

*H*ave you ever considered that you are a star people can touch? Does your presence light up a room when you enter? Do your children and grandchildren reflect back to you the love you give them? Do the elderly say you make a difference in their lives? Yes, you can become a star in so many areas of life…if you will only think in larger terms.

We each have 24 hours a day, 7 days a week. What are you going to do with yours? All of the great conquests of life have started as a little idea in someone's head. It's what is done with that idea that counts. What are the deepest dreams you have? Maybe writing a song, starting a business, authoring a book, helping children, creating a new recipe? Reach out today and plan how you are going to energize that thought into reality. Don't let it fall to the ground and perish. Nurture and water it until the sunlight makes it grow.

We are elevated by our constant aspirations. Scripture says that without a vision a nation will perish—and so will we. As Christians, we either grow or we slide backward in our faith. No one advances by accident; all achievements are reached by a dream set into motion through actions.

* * * * *

Lord, I love to look into the vastness of space to see the twinkle of Your stars. Help me see them as motivation to reflect Your light in every aspect of my life so people will see You in me. Give me dreams and help me achieve them so I can glorify You. Amen.

Is Your Glass Half Full?

God saw all that He had made, and behold,
it was very good. And there was evening and
there was morning, the sixth day.

GENESIS 1:31

As we look online, in the media, or even in our own downtowns and neighborhoods, we are bound to get the idea that bad things can and do happen. These are hard times. People we know, strangers we have yet to meet, and even our families are going through trials. It's important to not take bits and pieces of information or the weight of our private circumstance and decide that the world is falling apart. God has the world in hand. God has you in hand. He will take from you all the burdens you carry today if you will give them to Him. This freedom allows you the opportunity to experience goodness and the hope of what God will do as He transforms today's trouble into something redeemable and even joy filled.

There's a story of a young boy who was on top of a pile of horse manure digging as fast and as hard as he could. His father, seeing his son work so hard on a pile of smelly waste, asked, "Weston, what are you doing on that pile of horse manure?" Weston replied, "Daddy, with this much horse manure, there must be a pony here somewhere!" This son certainly had his glass half full. You too can choose to be positive. There is goodness in everything—if we will only look for it.

* * * * *

Father, thank You for helping me be a positive person. I appreciate You giving me the ability to be an encourager to those around me. It certainly makes life much more exciting. Amen.

In Everything, Not for Everything

*In everything give thanks; for this is
God's will for you in Christ Jesus.*

1 THESSALONIANS 5:18

One evening we received two telephone calls that really put today's verse to the test. One was regarding a 15-year-old boy who had just been hospitalized. He was beginning a grueling chemotherapy regimen to combat newly diagnosed cancer. The second call was regarding a mother who went into the hospital for a hysterectomy. The doctors, in performing a routine biopsy, discovered cervical cancer.

How do we say "Thank You, God" for tragedies and sudden crises that threaten to destroy our personal worlds? I struggled with this question until I realized that this passage says "*in* everything." Well, "*in* everything" is not the same as "*for* everything." We don't give thanks for evil or for its tragic results. And at some time or another, we all come face-to-face with evil or an unexpected crisis that threatens us or our families. At such times, no mother can be thankful for the evil that threatens her loved ones, but she can and must be thankful to the God who oversees all that comes her way.

Even in the midst of our pain, God is always at work. We can remain grateful throughout our ordeal because we live in Jesus Christ and know that God cares for us even more than we care for our own children. God is the only perfect parent—and in Him we can find refuge in the day of trouble. Through every circumstance that comes our way, God continues to transform us into the image of His Son.

The art of successful living is to seek out thankfulness in all of life's events—to see positive meaning in *every* challenge and trust that God will work every adversity to our ultimate good.

* * * * *

Father God, may Your will be done in my life today and every day. Help me give thanks "in everything." Help me to look closely to find the good in all that You do and allow. Amen.

Treasure Life

I came that [people] may have life,
and have it abundantly.
JOHN 10:10

During my years of battling cancer, I renewed my zeal to treasure life. Through stretches of chemotherapy and other treatments, I watched as children, women, and men of all ages faced similar trials. This time of perseverance, this season of depending on the Lord like never before, led me toward a deeper appreciation of life. Now, each morning when I awaken, there is a new freshness to the day. Each evening as I put my head on the pillow I am so grateful to God for His goodness to me.

The other day my daughter, Jenny, shared with me something I wasn't aware of:

> Mom, you and Dad have always used the phrase "how blessed and thankful we are for where we are in life." But, Mom, it wasn't always good news. Yet you both have been so great about saying how well God provides. In the future, my own family is going to be more verbal with the terms "blessed" and "thankful." Thanks, Mom, for showing me how to have more gratitude.

What joy to receive such a comment from my daughter. I truly believe we are to treasure life to the fullest. Too often we take this incredible gift of life for granted. Appreciation for everything—minor and major—puts things in perspective and allows us to live more abundant lives. When we feel grateful, it affects our whole being. All the trivial issues fall away. I've discovered that often there is a laugh at the end of the rainbow.

* * * * *

Father God, thank You for a treasured life. I love life and want to live it more abundantly in You. You have given me a grateful heart, and I want to lift up others with this attitude. Amen.

Notice the Shadows of His Wings

How precious is your constant love,
O God! All humanity takes refuge in
the shadow of your wings.
PSALM 36:7 TLB

As a young girl, I loved to look down at the sidewalk on a bright sunny day and see the shadows of the clouds and planes as they passed by overhead. Living in a warm climate, I appreciated the big clouds because they blocked out the sun's hot rays and gave some relief from the heat. I can only imagine what kind of shadow God's wings would cast.

I know it would be much larger than that of a sparrow and even larger than a bald eagle or California condor. I can almost feel the cool shade under His wings. I'm so glad I can relax in His care and protection.

When life becomes busy or hard, I've been able to feel God's presence by being still and knowing that He is God. When you encounter seasons of hardship or chaos, don't forget to look toward heaven and see His big puffy clouds or look down and pay attention to the shadows on the sidewalk. Make the time for these moments and marvel at God's creativity. You will feel the great comfort of His covering.

* * * * *

Father God, thank You for reminding me to take the time to revel in the shadows of Your wings. Amen.

My Lord, Hear Me Now

Always be joyful. Always keep on praying. No matter what happens, always be thankful, for this is God's will for you who belong to Christ Jesus.

1 Thessalonians 5:16-18 TLB

God gives us the same love as He gives His Son Jesus Christ. And since we are children of God, our prayers won't be denied. Since we abide in Him, He listens! Oh how we all want to be confident of this power and assurance in our prayers. We need not waver in our faith because God is always with us!

What would our churches and families be like if we knew God in such a powerful way? We long to have the mind of God. He is so much greater than we are or ever will be. We realize there are many barriers to our having this kind of confident power in our prayers. Daily we must break down and eliminate hindrances to our walk with the Lord.

Each of us has different barriers. Whatever they are, we must be willing to come to grips with them and say, "Hindrances, get behind me!" Scripture is so very clear that we are to continually abide in Christ if our prayers are to speedily go to the throne for action. As we arise each day and as we recline each evening after a full day, we are to pray with joy. Prayer is not an irksome duty! As we pray with pure hearts and joy, God says to us, "Ask and you will receive, so that your joy may be made full" (John 16:24).

Our goal each day is to get to know our Lord better than we knew Him yesterday. Make it your priority to spend time with God daily. There's not a single right time or correct place. The only requirement is your willing heart.

* * * * *

Father God, You truly are a 24/7 God. Thank You for being here when I need You. Thank You for knowing everything I need or desire before I do. And thank You for allowing my weaknesses to glorify Your mighty strength. Amen.

Don't Fear Your Limits

You are merciful and gentle, Lord, slow in getting angry,
full of constant loving kindness and of truth.
PSALM 86:15 TLB

We humans tend to put great expectations on ourselves. We think if we don't meet a certain performance level, God will judge us. We tend to grade ourselves with negative points if we do this or if we don't do that. But God understands our limits. He knows our struggles before they even transpire. God knows how much pressure and stress we can endure. And with this awareness, He knows how much grace, mercy, and strength will be required to heal our wounds and restore us to Him. Since we are all uniquely made in His image, He knows us very well.

During various trials of life, we need to be reminded that He cares for us. Remember, nothing happens to us that isn't first approved by our heavenly Father. He is molding us into the image of Christ. We can handle everything that comes our way with His help.

・　・　・　・　・

Lord, thank You for screening out all those things I
can't handle. Give me the power to endure every situation that comes my way. Amen.

Trust Him for Everything

*As for me, I trust in You, O LORD, I say, "You are
my God." My times are in Your hand.*

PSALM 31:14-15

Why are some people healed and others not? Why
do some people get miracles while others pray
just as hard and every bit as sincerely but remain ill or even
die from disease? After endless months and years of petition-
ing God, I've come to realize that "God's will" will be done.
And His will is always good.

God has a perfect plan and timetable for each of us. The
sooner we recognize this in our Christian walks, the quicker
we'll understand that His thoughts and His ways are greater
than our own. Yes, God healed me of my mantle cell lym-
phoma, and I give Him praise for that. From the very beginning I claimed John 11:4 as my theme verse: "This sickness
is not to end in death, but for the glory of God, so that the
Son of God may be glorified by it."

What amazing peace I received when I turned this dra-
matic situation over to God. Bob and I agreed that through
this valley God was going to be glorified. That declaration
grew out of years and years of prayers and diligent study of
God's Word and His promises. We came to understand—
and prove—that we could trust God for everything. Yes,
even for our very lives.

No matter how circumstances appeared on the surface, we were convinced God was working out all things for His glory and our personal interest. This kind of faith makes life so exciting. We don't have to search the world for the purpose of life; we've found it and live it daily. The Westminster Confession of Faith expresses our goal very clearly: "Man's chief end is to glorify God and enjoy Him forever."

Prayer helps us establish this purpose in a profound and deeply personal way. Without the wondrous gift of prayer, how could we ever gain the sense that our lives on earth have meaning? We couldn't. We would be in that last and desolate state described by the apostle Paul: "without hope and without God" (Ephesians 2:12 NIV).

We essentially have two choices. We can pray or we can lose heart. Scripture tells us often that we should always pray and not give up (Luke 18:1). You and I can live lives marked by faith and hope or we can surrender to lives filled with fear, anxiety, worry, and despair. Let's choose to give praise to God because we have His strong arms around us! We cry out to Him because—in Jesus—He calls out to us. When life seems overwhelming, God wants us to lift our hands to Him as His little children wanting to be held in His loving arms. We may not even know what's wrong or why we feel heavyhearted or afraid. And we don't have to know. All we really need to know is where to turn.

When we face the many pressures of life, there is only one effective, successful way "through it all"—we are to pray.

Prayer is our way to the place of power, our path to the solutions for life's indecipherable dilemmas. Unbearable pressures need not be withstood by us when God's strong and willing shoulders are ready to bear them.

* * * * *

Dependable Father God, let me lean on You and trust Your promises for my life. You are the same in the past, present, and future. You never change. I praise Your steadfastness. Amen.

Inspiration for Your Quiet Moments

❧ ❧ ❧

Teatime Is Quiet Time

*A*nyone who knows me knows that tea just has to be a part of this book. I love everything tea related. The selection, preparation, and sipping of tea helps us slow down and delight in life. When was the last time you brewed a pot of your favorite tea or tried a new flavor to be savored?

Make tea the centerpiece of your time of stillness. Breathe in the scent of tea as it brews. Pour it gently into a pretty cup or one that reminds you of a particular time or person. Settle in your prayer nook for today's quiet moment with the Lord and sip your tea with gratitude. Lift up words of praise and worship with each lift of the cup to your lips. Experience the beauty of the moment.

Engraved on Your Heart

Her children arise and call her blessed;
her husband also, and he praises her.

PROVERBS 31:28 NIV

The famous thirty-first chapter of Proverbs is a portrait of the kind of godly woman I want to be. She is hardworking, nurturing, and creative. She has a good business sense as well as a finely tuned sense of balance. She delights in her roles as wife and mother. Most important, she fears the Lord. And what is her reward for her efforts? Her children and her husband call her blessed and praise her!

Such a reward would warm any woman's heart. I know I love it when my Bob and my children praise me and call me blessed! But I am also aware that many of you are godly women who pattern your life after biblical principles but do not receive praise from anyone. Many times you may feel or say, "What's the use? No one appreciates me."

Oh, there have been times in my life when I haven't felt appreciated, but God has helped me and taught me through those void periods. I realized that God was dealing with me about my motivations and expectations. He wanted me to do what I did to please Him, not my husband or my children or anyone else. When I stopped expecting people to react in certain ways, I began to act out of proper motivation.

I was aiming to please God, not expecting rewards from family and friends.

Do you know what began to happen? I stopped expecting praise from my family, but I started getting it! Praise came about when my family members were free to be themselves. Also, I discovered that I'm not nearly as hungry for compliments as I once was. I find I am satisfied because I am becoming more used to responding in a godly way to life and its many situations. I have become more aware of who I am—God's child—and why I am here—to grow closer to Him and learn His way of doing things. In the process, I have become far less dependent on people to feel worthwhile.

• • • • •

Lord, help me come to You for my sense of self and value. With each day, may I honor You with my actions, words, and decisions. And may I speak of Your goodness with affection, awe, and great gratitude. Amen.

Listen

*Everyone must be quick to hear, slow to
speak and slow to anger.*
JAMES 1:19

God in His great wisdom created mankind with two ears and one mouth. I'm sure that was because He wanted us to listen twice as much as we speak. Most of us are very poor listeners. Bob and I rate this skill as one of the top priorities in having a good relationship. I guarantee that if couples take the time to become better listeners, their relationships would be improved through better understanding and increased patience.

Women tend to be better listeners than men, probably because most men immediately want to fix what is broken, and many of them consider listening a waste of time. To them, the solution is what's important. They want to go directly to the bottom line.

Why not be brave and ask several of your trusted friends how they would rate your listening skills? Be prepared to take their honest answers and act upon the information constructively. Don't get into the trap of thinking you are much better at listening than so-and-so. Almost everyone is below par in this skill.

We will become better listeners when we realize how people value being heard. It gives people an awareness that we care for what they have to say and that we truly love them. Our own spirits are lifted up when those around us know we care for them.

Listening is truly an art form that can be mastered if we will practice. Observe yourself in a crowd or even one-on-one to see how you do. Change comes when you know the truth and are willing to take action.

* * * * *

God, I know that I get into trouble with my relationships when I stop listening and open my mouth. Please forgive me for the foolish words I have said over the years. Heal the wounds I have left behind. Help me improve my relationships by listening better. Let this begin today. Amen.

No More Tears

He will wipe every tear from their eyes. There will be no more death or mourning or crying or pain, for the old order of things has passed away.

REVELATION 21:4 NIV

Who else can give us a promise like this one? It's an exciting glimpse of what life in eternity with God will be like! Just think, no more tears, no more death, no more sorrow, no more crying! No more of the familiar, unavoidable pain of being human. These will disappear forever. Hard to imagine, isn't it? We live in a fallen and depraved world. As a result, our lives are often dysfunctional. Pain and unhappiness are familiar to all of us, regardless of what our position in life might be. Some have illnesses, some have money troubles, and some agonize over disrupted relationships.

But those who follow Christ won't live like this forever. We have God's promise on that. Someday all our pain will be wiped away, never to be experienced again. I look forward with great anticipation to that heavenly event. I hope you will be in heaven with me!

• • • • •

Lord, shine through me this day. Let the light of Your righteousness, Your strength, and Your truth reflect to all the people around me. Shine, Jesus, shine! Amen.

Live in the Present

*Do not be worried about your life, as to what you will
eat or what you will drink; nor for your body, as to
what you will put on. Is not life more than food,
and the body more than clothing?*

MATTHEW 6:25

As I've observed my five grandchildren over the years, one thing stands out very vividly—their ability to live and enjoy the moment. I have become so interested in how they can take the "now" and make it a present. As I get older, I'm trying to forget about what happened yesterday and what might happen tomorrow and, instead, just experience the fullness of today.

To capture the essence of the present, we need to give less attention to worries, mistakes, what's going wrong, general concerns, things to get done, the past, the future, and the undone. "Today I will only think about today. No regrets for the past or worry about future maybes." When you do this, your focus is on the now. You can smile, laugh, pray, think, and enjoy what the moment brings. At the beach, in the mountains, cleaning house, cooking a meal, and playing in the sandbox with a grandchild—that's where I find purpose and enjoyment. Often our anxieties are about situations we have no control over. I told the ladies at my seminars that 85 percent of the things we worry about never happen. So why spend all that negative energy on something that probably won't occur?

When we begin to see and experience the minute right now, we will begin to see the grandeur of God and His vastness. As we focus on the present, we will spend less time worrying about tomorrow. Become as a little child and enjoy the moment right now.

· · · · ·

Father God, block out yesterday and don't let me try to glimpse tomorrow. I want to make a present out of today. Help me see all You have given me right now, right this moment. May today be the greatest day of my life because I've enjoyed every minute of it. Amen.

Make a Date for Quietude

*There is an appointed time for everything. And there is
a time for every event under heaven.*

ECCLESIASTES 3:1

What would we do without our day planners? I have a large one for my desk and a carry-all that goes with me everywhere. I don't know how a person functions without some type of organizer. I just love it! It truly has become my daily-calendar bible. My entire life is represented in that book. Each evening I peek in to see what tomorrow has to bring. I just love to see a busy calendar; it makes me feel so alive. I've got this to do and that to do.

Then I come upon a day that has all white space. Not one thing to do. "Oh what will I do to fill all that space and time?" I wonder. That's the way I used to think and plan. All my spaces had appointments written down, and many times they even overlapped. I was almost afraid of white spaces. But now I build in white spaces. I even plan ahead weeks or months and black out "saved for me or my family" days. I have realized that there are precious times for my loved ones and me. Bob and I protect saved spaces just for us. We may not go anywhere or do anything out of the ordinary, but it's our special time together. We can do anything we want: sleep in, stay out late, go to lunch, read a book, go to a movie, or take a nap. I look forward with great anticipation to these white spaces appearing on my calendar.

I've been so impressed when I've read biographies of famous people. Many of them are controllers of their own time. They don't let outsiders dictate their schedules. Sure, there are times when things have to be done on special days, but generally that isn't the case. When we control our calendars, we will find that our lives are more enjoyable and that the tensions of life are more manageable. Make those white spaces your friend, not your enemy.

* * * * *

Father, let me be at peace when I see those blank spaces on my calendar. May I be so bold as to create my own white spaces. I know that my body needs to be recharged, and those free times can be great for my spiritual, mental, and physical well-being. Amen.

A Time for Everything

[God] has made everything beautiful in its time.
ECCLESIASTES 3:11 NIV

Ralph Waldo Emerson said it so well: "Finish every day and be done with it. You have done what you could. Some blunders and absurdities no doubt crept in; forget them as soon as you can. Tomorrow is a new day; begin it well and serenely and with too high a spirit to be cumbered with old nonsense. This day is all that is good and fair. It is too dear, with its hopes and invitations, to waste a moment on yesterday."

Truly there is a season for everything. Behind every happening, there is a purpose. Nothing happens by accident. Life flows through its natural cycles. There is a time to be born—a beginning, and a time to die—an ending. God has a divine timetable. When my mother-in-law passed away, we were richly blessed by knowing that her cycle of life on earth had been completed as God planned. We knew that through the years, God had turned every ugly event in her life beautiful. And now she was trading her earthly life for one in which there was no more pain.

During her life she had heartaches and laughter, along with sickness and health. There were no "whys" asked when she passed away. We knew that it was part of God's cycle.

When we realize that God has a timing for everything, we can trust that everything will be beautiful in His perfect time.

* * * * *

Lord of time and life, You are the alpha and the omega. You are the beginning and the end. Help me be patient and learn to live at peace with Your timetable. Let me not rush my agenda. I want to trust You more. Amen.

Look at Anger

A wise man restrains his anger and overlooks insults. This is to his credit.
PROVERBS 19:11 TLB

A healthy relationship cannot exist where anger exists. The two do not go together. For healthy relationships and friendships to flourish, we must be willing and able to control the raging fire that exists in all of us to some degree. The book of Proverbs gives some insights concerning anger:

- A short-tempered man is a fool. He hates the man who is patient (Proverbs 14:17 TLB).

- A quick-tempered man starts fights; a cool-tempered man tries to stop them (15:18).

- It is better to be slow-tempered than famous; it is better to have self-control than to control an army (16:32).

- A fool gets into constant fights. His mouth is his undoing! His words endanger him (18:6-7).

- A short-tempered man must bear his own penalty; you can't do much to help him. If you try once you must try a dozen times (19:19).

- Keep away from angry, short-tempered men, lest you learn to be like them and endanger your soul (22:24-25).

- A rebel shouts in anger; a wise man holds his temper in and cools it (29:11).

- There is more hope for a fool than for a man of quick temper (29:20).

- A hot-tempered man starts fights and gets into all kinds of trouble (29:22).

If anger is one of your enemies, go to God in prayer and ask for healing. Unrighteous anger is a cancer that can destroy your body if not addressed. Don't wait until it is too late. Healthy relationships demand that anger be conquered.

* * * * *

God, help me examine myself to see if there is any evidence of unrighteous anger in my life. If so, help me deal with it and turn it over to You. Amen.

Clear Out Your Prayer Closet

In the early morning, while it was still dark,
Jesus got up, left the house, and went away to a
secluded place, and was praying there.
MARK 1:35

Every so often, we need to evaluate what's happening in our prayer lives. This way we can catch ourselves if we're slipping in our purpose and direction. Sometimes our prayers and methods become routine—not much is happening that is really meaningful. Maybe the hinges to your prayer closet door are rusty, but they do open and shut at their appointed times. Perhaps the doors are locked and cobwebbed. Or maybe you don't neglect prayer itself, but what a tale the walls might tell: "We have heard you when you have been in such a rush that you could hardly spend two minutes with God. We have witnessed you coming and spending ten minutes and not asking for anything—at least your heart didn't ask. The lips moved, but the heart was silent. We have heard you groan out of your soul, but we have seen you go away distrustful, not believing your prayer was heard, quoting the promise, but not thinking God would fulfill it."

We can find ourselves going through the motions of prayer but not really praying. It's sort of like driving down the freeway at 65 miles per hour and not remembering the landscape that has whizzed by. We need to slow down and clear out the cobwebs from our minds as we kneel before God. He deserves our utmost awareness as we come before Him. Get excited about prayer time! Pay attention, be alert, and stay awake.

* * * * *

God, may I go beyond the language of formal prayer, to seek the spirit of prayer. May You bless me and honor my supplications. Amen.

God Is Bound by His Promises

Keep watching and praying that you may
not enter into temptation; the spirit
is willing, but the flesh is weak.
MATTHEW 26:41

God always keeps His promises. His character will not let Him fail. In truth, all prayers offered through His Son, Jesus, are going to be heard. God finds joy in keeping His Word.

God's actions are always consistent with His character, including His love, righteousness, holiness, and justice. He cannot lay aside any of His attributes and act independently of it. It is part of His being to be just. In all of His actions, God acts with fairness. If He did less, He would no longer be God! Deuteronomy 32:4 says, "The Rock! His work is perfect, for all His ways are just; a God of faithfulness and without injustice, righteous and upright is He."

We live in a day where all aspects of life are being undermined by dishonesty. Families have lost most of their retirement funds because they believed executives' promises that were made with their fingers crossed behind their backs. Oh, how desperate our country is for people with solid character! We look to our sports heroes, our political leaders, our corporate leadership, the stars of movies and television, and even our spiritual leaders, hoping they will show us how people of good character live. Each time we feel comfortable that a certain personality has the answer, we are disappointed by a revelation of broken dreams and promises.

We expect people to do what they say they are going to do. We are disappointed when plumbers, electricians, painters, or coworkers fail to do or even can't do what they've said they are going to do. They miss an appointment or don't deliver a product on time—and here we are patiently waiting and nothing happens. Even parents tell their children that such-and-such will happen on Saturday, and it doesn't happen as promised. How many children go to their rooms to cry because a promise was broken?

I am so thankful I have One who never goes back on His promises. God the Father, Jesus the Son, and the Holy Spirit—the holy trinity—always keeps His word. If God says it, we can believe it. Let's all learn from the Master of character to do what we say we're going to do.

* * * * *

Beloved Father, thanks for being a promise keeper. You are the model for every woman who wants to be honorable, including me. You give me great confidence in Your Word because I know You never break Your promises. If You said it, I believe it. Amen.

Too Much to Do

*We hear that some among you are leading
an undisciplined life, doing no work at all,
but acting like busybodies.*

2 THESSALONIANS 3:11

Too many things on your to-do list today? Are you overwhelmed with children, housework, husband, laundry, meal preparation, work, marketing, and the multitude of things it takes to run your life and household? Has your pursuit of the daily routine left you with no prayer time, no time for Bible study, and no time for just a few moments of quiet reflection? I know what it's like when that which your heart craves—fellowship with God—just doesn't seem to fit into the schedule. And yet the busier we are, the more we need to be spiritually fit to meet the day's demands.

As a young mom with five children under five, it was difficult for me to put God first, but when I did, my days went so much better. I was able to have a peaceful heart and a sweeter spirit. It was much more likely that the priorities of my day would fall into place after even a brief time spent with the Lord. My day was brightened when I took time to praise God for my family and for His love. The psalmist wrote,

Because your love is better than life, my lips will glorify you. I will praise you as long as I live, and in your name I will lift up my hands. I will be fully satisfied as with the richest of foods; with singing lips my mouth will praise you (Psalm 63:3-5 NIV).

Today with grown children and five grandchildren, I can see even more clearly what's really important in life. It's that quiet time when I get to know God's Word, pray God's Word, and walk in God's Word and His promises.

Don't make the mistake of getting so busy you don't have time for God. The less time you spend in God's Word, the more time you spend on yourself.

· · · · ·

Lord, make me aware of the important issues of life. Make my desire to be with You a reality. I want to be a mom and grandmom who honors You. Amen.

Conformed Versus Transformed

Do not be conformed to this world, but be transformed
by the renewing of your mind, so that you may
prove what the will of God is, that which is
good and acceptable and perfect.

ROMANS 12:2

*H*ave you ever asked, "What is the will of God for my life?" I know I have many times. This question seems like the biggest mystery of the Christian walk. How do I know that? Well, I have used this passage as a help to make me realize that there is a tremendous battle going on in my mind between good and evil, right and wrong, godly and ungodly. This verse is a reminder regarding that battle. I always want to be in God's will and not my own. I must open my mind to realize that the world (secular thinking) is trying to win me over to its side. However, the warning in Romans is not to be conformed, but to be *transformed* by the renewing of my mind so that I can:

- know what the will of God is
- learn what is good, acceptable, and perfect

A companion verse to help me in this transformation of the mind is found in Philippians 4:8, which reads: "Whatever is true, whatever is honorable, whatever is right, whatever is pure, whatever is lovely, whatever is of good repute, if there is any excellence and if anything worthy of praise, dwell on these things."

I assure you that if you use these two verses, and if you study the Scriptures, your mind will be transformed and you'll know what the will of God is for your life. Don't forget to talk to well-respected Christians and pastors too. Their insights can be very helpful. Formulate your direction and move out in faith. Because you are earnestly seeking God's will, if you are going in the wrong direction, He will correct your course.

* * * * *

Father God, I cherish the various verses of Scripture You encourage me to put in my heart so I can be drawing closer to You all the time. I'm glad You've given me a desire for goodness so I can honor You. Amen.

Worship

*Come let us worship and bow down, let us
kneel before the LORD our Maker.*

PSALM 95:6

As people read the book of Psalms, they began to study
the various forms of worship. As we look at the various denominations around us, we can see how the founders
of each one established ways to worship by what they perceived after reading this great book in the Bible. Over the
centuries, Christian worship has taken many forms, involving various expressions and postures on the part of churchgoers. The psalms portray worship as an act of the complete
person, not just his or her mental sphere.

The Hebrew word for "worship" literally means "to kneel"
or "to bow down." The act of worship is the gesture of humbling oneself before a higher authority. The psalms also tell
us to "sing to the LORD, bless His name" (96:2). Music has
played a large part in this sacred facet of worship. Physical gestures and movements are also mentioned. Lifting our
hands before God signifies our loyalty to Him. Clapping our
hands is representative of our celebrating before God. Some
worshipers rejoice in His presence with timbrel (a small hand
drum or tambourine) and dancing (Psalm 150:4).

To worship like the psalmist advocates is to obey Jesus' command to "love the Lord your God with all your heart, and with all your soul, and with all your mind, and with all your strength" (Mark 12:30). There are several more insights for worship found in the book of Psalms:

- God's gifts of instruments and vocal music should be used to help us worship (Psalm 47:1; 81:1-4; 150).

- We can appeal to God for help and know He hears us (4:3).

- We can thank Him for His deliverance (17:1-5).

- Difficult times should not prevent us from praising God (22:23-24; 102:1-2; 140:4-8).

- We are to celebrate what God has done for us (18; 106; 136).

- Confessing our sins relieves us of many burdens (32; 42:5-11; 116).

* * * * *

Father God, thank You for giving us the great book of Psalms, the wonderful book of praise. There are so many ways to worship You. May I always stay open to these ways so I never think my way alone is perfect. May all forms be acceptable to You. Amen.

Inspiration for Your Quiet Moments

❧ ❧ ❧

Stillness Beneath the Stars

Select an evening that will offer a clear view to the stars, and plan ahead to make it a time of talking to God. Have a sleeping bag or big blanket ready, along with a flashlight if you have to walk out to a special spot. You might be lucky enough to have a porch ideal for stargazing or, even better, a tree house. Anyplace you can take in the majestic heavens will do. It might be the corner window of your living room if your 10-story apartment building offers such a vista. Make your date with the stars. God will be ready and waiting to hear all you have to say to Him as you wish, dream, and pray while looking at the sparkling stars.

Why not invite your family to this quiet time and start a tradition? Teach your little ones to speak straight to the heavens. And if you have teens who don't open up very much, extend the invitation and make room on the blanket for them. It's hard to resist relaxing and having a good time during an evening under the stars. Start the time with a simple prayer to set the quiet tone or ask each person to share what his or her prayer for the night is. Make it an evening to remember.

A New Heart

I will give you one heart and a new spirit;
I will take from you your hearts of stone and give
you tender hearts of love for God.

EZEKIEL 11:19

The number one killer in America is heart failure. Americans tend to place tremendous stress on that fist-sized muscle. Some of the stress on our hearts is caused by the food we eat, our high-pressure lifestyles, and our lack of physical exercise. Other health problems can stress our hearts as well. And some hearts—such as those with congenital defects—are less able to handle stress.

Spiritually speaking, we are all born with a congenital heart problem—sin. We are all sinners and prone to rebel against God's plans for our lives. The more we continue on our own way, the more hardened and scarred our spiritual hearts become. But we don't have to live that way. God promises that He will give us new hearts and new spirits. And His transformation is done without needles and anesthesia.

He will replace your hardened old heart with a tender, loving one. To take advantage of this wonderful opportunity, all you have to do is surrender your heart to Him by accepting His Son Jesus Christ as your Lord and Savior. Why wait?

. . . . .

Sweet Jesus, I know I have sinned and lived according to my rules and not Yours. I know You came to earth, died on the cross to cover my sins, and rose again to conquer death. Thank You! I renounce my sins and accept You as my Lord and Savior. Help me learn more about You so I can honor and worship You in everything I do from this time forth. Amen.

Good to Be Alone

*For the Lord God…says: "Only in returning to me
and waiting for me will you be saved; in quietness
and confidence is your strength."*
ISAIAH 30:15 TLB

One of the great virtues of the Christian life is learning
how to appreciate solitude. As our society gets more
technologically advanced, it is becoming more difficult to
be alone. You can't go to a movie anymore without being
shaken out of your seat by the loud blasting of special effects.
Music has become so loud that it hurts our ears. We're on call
24/7 with our smart phones, tablets, and computers.

Many times, God's most meaningful touches on our
lives come when we are all alone. I have journeyed through
major illness, and one of the blessings of facing such a physical trial is that it gives us an opportunity to be alone. I've
been able to revisit some of the big issues of life while I've
lain in my bed recuperating from treatments. God provided
this sweet time—just between Him and me.

Don't wait for illness to occur; schedule time to be
alone with God today. Take time to go for a long walk in
the mountains, in the woods, or by the beach and be alone
with Your creator. Schedule a time just as you would a business appointment. Some of my most creative times happen

when I'm alone with God, and I'm sure the same will be
true for you.

* * * * *

*Lord God, our quiet times alone together are some of
my most precious experiences. I cherish my time with
You. Amen.*

A Light
in the Dark

She gets up while it is still night;
she provides food for her family and
portions for her female servants.
PROVERBS 31:15 NIV

When I spoke with hundreds of women every year, I found they were often struggling to find the answers to the same two questions: "Who am I?" and "Why am I here?" If God's answers to these two questions of life are not yet engraved on your heart, I pray that you will set out on a journey to discover His responses and then rest in His purposes for you.

Go to Scripture, talk to a godly friend, attend a Bible-teaching church, set aside part of each day to talk to God in prayer. If you seek sincerely, God will show you the traits of the godly woman He created you to be. Then step out in obedience, depending on Jesus. As you do, the beauty of godliness will shine in your life.

As women, we have the wonderful opportunity to let our lives sparkle with God's love—if we let Him in. Almighty God is our guide and shepherd. He will give us the spirit of godliness to complete our search for who we are, why we're here, and how we can help others.

* * * * *

Father God, You give me hope and purpose. May I discover Your will for my life and then enthusiastically pursue it. Amen.

Walking with Integrity

The righteous lead blameless lives;
blessed are their children after them.
PROVERBS 20:7 NIV

My Bob often says, "Just do what you say you are going to do!" This has been our battle cry for more than 50 years. People get into relational problems because they forget to keep their promises. It's so easy to make a verbal promise for the moment, and then later grapple with the execution of that agreement.

Sometimes we underestimate the consequences of not keeping a promise made in a moment of haste. Many times we aren't even aware that we have made a promise. Someone says, "I'll call you at seven tonight," or "I'll drop by before noon," or "I'll call you to set up a breakfast meeting on Wednesday." We take that to mean a promise, but the person speaking doesn't. Then the weak excuses follow when the person doesn't follow through. "I got tied up and forgot." "I was too tired." Or, even worse, a lie is told "I called but no one answered" (even though no message was left on voice mail).

Let's not make promises if we aren't going to keep them. That will help us and the person on the receiving end. Yes, there will be times when the execution of a promise will have to be rescheduled, but be up front with the person when you call to change the time frame. We aren't perfect and we can't control everything, but we can model good relationship skills to our friends and family by exhibiting accountability when we give our word. We teach people that we are trustworthy, and how they can become trustworthy too when we walk with integrity.

You'll be surprised at how people will be pleasantly surprised when you keep your promises. When you develop a reputation for being a woman who does what she says, your life will have more meaning and people will enjoy being around you.

· · · · ·

Father, I want to be a person people can trust. Let me examine my words before I speak them to make sure I only give promises that I can follow through on. Keeping promises reflects who I am in You. Help me to be true to my words. Amen.

Have the Right Perspective

You are my refuge and my shield, and your
promises are my only source of hope.
Psalm 119:114 tlb

People have asked me how I could be so upbeat when so many things around me were negative during my time of cancer treatments. I guess it's because of my perspective on life. Through Scripture and life experiences, I have come to trust that God has a master plan for my life. He knew me from the beginning of time. He knows my beginning and He knows the end. He is the alpha and the omega. Because He has taken care of me in the past, and He is taking care of me in the present, I have the assurance that He will take care of my future. A long time ago I told God, "Your will be done in my life." And I meant it with my whole heart.

God's Word gives me much comfort too. I read His Word to be reminded of His promises and that I can count on Him to follow through. When I face troubles that seem insurmountable to me, I have a hope that is powerful and limitless. My hope in the Lord is absolute. When the psalmist tells me that God is my shield and that His promises and His Word are my source of hope, I believe it. God's character is one of honor, trust, and reliability that I can bank on.

God's Word brings me light on foggy days. It brings me hope when I become discouraged, and it helps me not to make a mountain out of a molehill. His Word gives me the right perspective—His perspective—on my life. I know my time on earth is such a short time and my time with Him after this earthly experience will be for eternity.

. . . . .

Father God, thank You for sharing with me Your wisdom that gives me hope for today and tomorrow. Your Word provides the framework that allows me to keep going even when times are hard. When I begin to fret and worry, let me see my situation with Your eternal perspective. Amen.

Three Sweet Words

Beloved, let us love one another, for love is from God;
and everyone who loves is born of God and knows God.

1 John 4:7

Have you hungered after love? When my father, who was an alcoholic, was alive I hoped he would come home with love in his heart rather than the anger he often exhibited. As a young girl, I would have so cherished these three big words: "I love you." I guess that's one of the first reasons I was so attracted to my Bob. He came from a warm family that was very free in their expressions of endearment.

Over the years I too have made it a habit to say "I love you" frequently. Saying these words that can be difficult (people in the world find them so hard to utter) has been very beneficial. They help me feel good inside and they bless the receivers. The words also help me realize that I'm a giver, not just a taker.

When our loved ones hear these words they certainly help mitigate any mistakes or missteps we've made with them recently. I often catch myself saying "I love you" as I hang up from talking to a family member or friend. And you know what? After a while they return the "I love you"! And our relationship takes on a warmer, softer, more caring tone. There are many opportunities during the day to express "I love you."

Individuals who know they are loved have a cheerier outlook on life. There is a sparkle in their eyes, and they can look people eye-to-eye with faces that reflect confidence and caring. This inner peace radiates in all of their relationships. It is most difficult to not like someone who sincerely says he or she loves you. In fact, I'd say it is impossible!

The Scriptures are quite clear that God is love, and when we don't love we don't know God intimately. How often have we known a person for a short time but instantly knew they were kindred spirits? Why? Because he or she radiated the love of God. God's light truly shines.

. . . . .

Father God, may I be known by those around me as a person who knows how to say "I love you." May my family welcome my words and learn to sincerely reflect them back to me and say them to the people who are important in their lives. Help me freely share these life-giving words based on Your love. Amen.

God's Grace Is Sufficient

*The Spirit helps us in our weakness. We do not know
what we ought to pray for, but the Spirit himself
intercedes for us through wordless groans.*
ROMANS 8:26 NIV

When I don't have the strength to utter words to heaven to express my desires, God hears my desires anyway. He understands even our groanings. Our tongues don't have to speak words before He hears them. Parents often know what's in their children's mind without them even talking. Likewise, a spouse often instantaneously knows what the other is thinking and oftentimes finishes a sentence of the mate. God is like this with us.

The Holy Spirit is the alpha and omega of our prayers. He knows the beginning and the end. He knows our hearts and can discern our troubles and our pleas even when we are struggling to know what to pray about specifically.

During many of my stays at hospitals during my cancer treatments, I often didn't know what to pray for. My Bob and I didn't always have the knowledge to really understand our situation. Oh, yes, we asked questions, but the explanations weren't decoded for our ears. Large multisyllable medical terms were too difficult for our ears to grasp. To be honest with you, there were times when we were too tired and stressed to even feel like praying.

However, during those void times, we knew God would redeem our energy and that He would give us the "right words" for the moment. Those were great prayer sessions! We entered with little and exited with joy and satisfaction. How could that be? We were so confused, but God gave us order.

Don't be fearful to pray when you feel the same way we felt. The Holy Spirit will renew your desire for prayer, and He will give you words to speak. God's grace is sufficient for all your needs.

. . . . .

God, just knowing that You will intercede for me when I don't have the power or words to ask for Your help is so reassuring. Thank You for knowing me that well and loving me that much. Amen.

Live Each Day to Its Fullest

Be filled with the Spirit...always giving thanks
for all things in the name of our Lord Jesus Christ
to God, even the Father.

EPHESIANS 5:18,20

Because of the cancer, I've spent a lot of time waiting in the reception areas of doctors' offices. (In most cases, the wait was at least an hour after my scheduled appointment.) During this time, I had the opportunity to talk to people who were diagnosed with diseases that shorten their life expectancies. In short, they have received the "bad news." In this course of events, I became aware that I no longer wanted to wait for bad news before I began to appreciate life. I've always been a thankful person with gratitude to God for what He has given me, but now I'm more dedicated to not taking for granted one single day of my existence because life can be very short. I don't want to postpone one day of thankfulness for the life I have. It is so precious.

Our situations can change at the drop of a hat. Bad news can come in a moment's notice. We have no promise from God that we will live forever; in fact, the Bible says, "It is appointed for men to die" (Hebrews 9:27). As I look around today, I truly thank God abundantly for the simple things of life: sleeping, walking, running, heartbeats, husband, children, grandchildren, peace, and so on. Things I used to take for granted. Now I never want to give in to the fear of what might come next…the fear of the unknown. I want to be grateful to God for all that He gives to me and my family. I find myself taking moments several times a day to thank God for all my blessings. I don't want to leave out even the most minute reason for appreciation.

I think that time of uncertainty was a wonderful experience for me because it made me appreciate what I have. I'm far more aware of how bountiful my life is and has been. I have a thankful heart because of that season in my life. My glass is truly half full, not half empty.

* * * * *

Lord, I don't want to wait to receive bad news before I thank You. Make me aware of all my blessings so that I see them with open eyes and a full heart, even during times of trials. You are the giver of all goodness, and I thank You for all Your provisions. Amen.

Like a Deer

The Lord God is my strength; he will give me the speed
of a deer and bring me safely over the mountains.

HABAKKUK 3:19 TLB

Deer are such beautiful animals. When I was a child, Walt Disney made Bambi come alive. My heart has always been tender toward deer. They are so agile and run at such speed, even on mountainous terrain.

I am blessed to know that God makes my feet as swift as a deer's and that He enables me to travel safely over higher plains. When we vacation in the mountains, Bob and I love to see the deer on the ridges across the valley. They run with such swiftness because their lungs are conditioned to race to the highest peak. That's the way I want my life to function. I want to run swiftly toward the mark and respond to the highest calling. God's strength is sufficient for me.

Just to know that my God is all-knowing and that He has power over everything gives me solace. This truth gives me such assurance that He is capable of doing what He says. I look forward to more adventures with Him!

. . . . .

Father God, what would I do without Your grace?
Humble me so that I might receive more of You. Break
me so that I can be made whole through Your Son
Jesus. Amen.

Check Your Power Source

*The Lord says, "I will make my people strong with
power from me!...Wherever they go they
will be under my personal care.*
ZECHARIAH 10:12 TLB

The other morning while preparing breakfast, I put two
pieces of bread in the toaster, pushed down the lever,
walked away to soft-boil my eggs, and returned in a few minutes to find my bread still in the toaster—but not toasted. I
scratched my head, pushed down the lever once again, but
this time I didn't walk away. I stayed close by to observe what
went wrong the first time. Again no toast, and no hot wires
visible inside the toaster. I asked Bob, "Why isn't my bread
toasting?"

Looking over my shoulder, my Bob said, "Have you ever
thought of plugging the cord into the socket?" Dumb is me!
Why would I expect toast when the appliance wasn't plugged
into the power source? Later that morning I reflected on
that situation at breakfast and then moved on to realizing
I don't get answers from God when I'm not plugged into
Him either.

In Southern California where we live, we have many
service companies that want to take care of our every need.
We have personal trainers, personal shoppers, home deco-
rators, animal groomers, valet parking, and guides for the

amusement parks. However, none of these services can take care of our spiritual needs. We need something much larger than a "service" can provide.

Since God has promised to make us strong with His power, we need to break out and take some control over our lives. God has given us many truths that enable us to make appropriate choices for proper and healthy living. When we are confronted with certain illnesses, as I have been, as well as many of you, we must rely on good common sense. Our intuition will give us insights on what needs to be done. We just need to make sure we're plugged into the right power source!

Remember, God is always looking over your shoulder. When He is needed, He is right with you! You are under His personal care at all times.

· · · · ·

Father, let me rely on Your power more. The weight that I'm carrying is too heavy. Help me to say no when I find myself trying to solve all my problems. I want to turn to You instead. Amen.

A Safe Refuge—Home

God is our refuge and strength, a very present help in
trouble. Therefore we will not fear, though the earth
should change and though the mountains slip into
the heart of the sea; though its waters roar and foam,
though the mountains quake at its swelling pride.

PSALM 46:1-3

God is a refuge in times of trouble, tumult, and turmoil.
In today's passage, the psalmist is saying, "When my
world becomes a worrisome, fearful place, I take refuge in
my God." God is a place of safety for His people. He always
has been, and He always will be. And I believe that a godly
home—a home where Jesus Christ is obeyed and honored—
becomes a physical refuge, a place where people worn down
by the noise, commotion, and hostility of the outside world
can find a safe place to rest. A welcoming home is a place
people enjoy coming to.

If you live in a house with small children, you may
already be shaking your head. "What do you mean 'noise,
commotion, and hostility of the outside world'? I have to
leave home to get away from the turmoil!" Believe me, I
understand. But even in the rough-and-tumble of family life,
home can be a safe haven and even a place of quiet (at least
some of the time). If you find noise and activity crowding

your family life and pushing and pulling at you, making the extra effort to create a sense of refuge in the midst of it can pay wonderful dividends.

Maybe this concept depends on how we define "refuge." I'm not talking about a hole we disappear down to eat and sleep and then emerge to go about the business of life. In *Youniquely Woman,* a book I wrote with Kay Arthur and Donna Otto, we talk about the home as a refuge and that a welcoming home is where real life happens. It's where personalities are nurtured, growth is stimulated, and people feel free to be who they are and yet also grow. That caring, nurturing quality—not the absence of noise or occasional strife—is what makes a home a refuge. As women, we are the thermostats of our homes. We are the ones who establish the atmosphere. God has built into us a desire to build a refuge and nest for our husband and children. If a refuge is going to be built, it will be through our efforts. A woman is fortunate if she is blessed with a husband who lends a hand to make this happen, but your heartbeat for your home will be the driving force behind establishing a place of peaceful rest.

It's best to not have any great expectations about anyone else helping you out in this project. And don't expect it to be done overnight. This is a lifetime project. Do it because you have been called to make that cozy nest for your loved ones. Besides, you will also receive a great benefit from having a cozy, charming refuge:

By wisdom a house is built, and by understanding it is established; and by knowledge the rooms are filled with all precious and pleasant riches (Proverbs 24:3-4).

* * * * *

Father God, give me a passion and desire to build a refuge for my family. Let me see the long-term rewards for all of us. Amen.

Keep Your Joy Alive

You have sorrow now, but I will see you again and then you will rejoice; and no one can rob you of that joy.
JOHN 16:22 TLB

Joy will follow sorrow. I've met so many women who are right in the middle of sorrow—a death, a separation, a divorce, a serious health problem, teenage children who are rebelling, financial difficulties, unbelieving mates, and the list goes on and on. Each of us, at one time or the other, has been in deep sorrow. Sometimes it seems like a smile will never appear on our faces again because the current load is so great.

At one time, between dealing with my illness and the heartache of my daughter's troubled marriage, my heart was so heavy. Tears of sorrow streamed down my face and soaked my pillow. As I prayed for those situations many times, I pleaded to God to "restore to me the joy of Your salvation" (Psalm 51:12). Then a friend would call or I'd receive a note through the mail or a fax with a verse of Scripture or an encouraging poem. The load became lighter, and God continued my joy even during my times of trouble.

In my Bible I have a card that reads, "Don't doubt in the morning what God has promised you in the night." My friend, don't let anyone or anything take away your joy. It is yours to have and to hold.

. . . . .

Father God, help me see Your beauty all around me.
May the cup of joy You offer spill over and touch me
and everyone around me. Joy is a decision on my part,
and I'm committed to You so no one can take it away
from me. Amen.

A Life of Blessings

*Blessed are the peacemakers, for they will
be called children of God.*

MATTHEW 5:9 NIV

History is full of people who have been peacemakers. They were willing to risk their well-being, health, and wealth to stand in the gap between separated parties to help end disagreements and avoid wars. Even within families we can witness the terrible destruction that takes place between warring members. Sometimes the road of life seems strewn with fragmented lives. But Jesus is quite clear that He wants *all* of His children to be known as peacemakers. Scripture makes it plain that we are to be known as ambassadors of peace:

- *God:* "God has given us the privilege of urging everyone to come into his favor and be reconciled to him" (2 Corinthians 5:18 TLB).

- *Ourselves:* "Joy fills hearts that are planning for good!" (Proverbs 12:20 TLB).

- *Others:* "And those who are peacemakers will plant seeds of peace and reap a harvest of goodness" (James 3:18 TLB).

Since the blessing of being a peacemaker is part of the call of being a child of God, we can experience the joy of goodness, happiness, and peace within our lives. When we exhibit these positive traits, we reflect:

- *Contentment with ourselves:* We know who we are in Christ, thus we have the contentment we've searched for.

- *Optimism in our faith:* We exhibit a love for God and reflect a positive faith in how we look at life and the events that come our way.

- *Relational connectedness:* We have deeper friendships. People will be bonded closer to us. We become better friends.

- *Mercy:* We are more willing and capable of being compassionate and lenient in our dealings with ourselves and others.

- *Doing what is right:* We have a benchmark to judge godly behavior for ourselves.

Make Jesus your Savior and become a peacemaker!

* * * * *

Dear Lord, may I have the courage to step out and become a peacemaker. Let peace and love start with me and ripple out to others I meet. Help me humble myself so I can be lifted up and used for Your kingdom. Amen.

Inspiration for Your Quiet Moments

❧ ❧ ❧

Delighting in Listening

Select a portion of Scripture to read for several days in a row. Consider a favorite psalm or a beloved chapter in the Gospels. During your quiet time, read a line or a sentence, and then just sit with it, mulling it over. Let the words sink in and give them space in your heart and mind. And then listen. What is God sharing about His character? His love? His compassion? His hope for you?

Often in our busy lives we approach reading the Bible as though it is a book to be finished rather than a message to be returned to again and again during every season of life. Listen to what the living Word of God offers your heart today.

Be Joyful

*[Jesus said,] "These things I have spoken to you
so that My joy may be in you, and that
your joy may be made full."*

JOHN 15:11

People like to be around individuals who radiate joy in their presence. And when someone has very little joy in their lives, they often have few friendships. Many times we expect the fruit of joy to bring us unlimited happiness and fun times. Yet when we read the Scriptures, we are encouraged to reflect on what it really means to have a joyful heart. Happiness and fun are good in themselves, but they come and go. Joy, however, is felt beyond our circumstances. Joy exists even when times are difficult because it is in an *attitude* we have toward life. It is a treasure of the heart—the comfort of knowing God's intimate presence. The Roman philosopher Aurelius said, "Find joy in simplicity, self-respect, and indifference to what lies between virtue and vice. Love the human race. Follow the divine."

As we view the events of our lives, we can choose to be resentful toward God for letting certain things happen to us or we can choose an attitude of gratitude and a commitment to joy. Joy is our best choice! We have joy when we are serving God and doing what He wants for our lives. We have joy when we learn to take circumstances and the ups and downs of life in stride and use all situations to bring glory to Jesus. We lighten our load in life and draw others to us by having joyful hearts. When we have joy in the Lord, we begin to see life from God's point of view. We realize that things have never looked so beautiful, so peaceful, so amazing. The joy of the Lord is truly our strength.

· · · · ·

God, thank You for giving me an attitude of joy. I can truly share that having a glass half full is more rewarding than having a glass that is half empty. Amen.

Celebrate Each Day

*Teach us to number our days and recognize how few
they are; help us to spend them as we should.*
Psalm 90:12 TLB

How often do we talk in terms of days? Usually our reference is in terms of years. She's 37 years old, they were married 15 years ago, I've been sober for 10 years. One thing about youth is that they think they have nine lives and they will never get old. They think they are "eternally young"! But as we get older, we realize that we are running out of years and our thoughts turn to the months and to the days.

Today's verse suggests that we are to "number our days." We are encouraged to live each day to the fullest so that when our lives draw to an end, we have spent each day as we should and gained "a heart of wisdom" (NIV). When we live each moment for the Lord, we live it with gusto and enthusiasm.

I've found that as I get older, the inevitables of life happen and I must learn to adjust to the unknowns that appear from time to time. We cannot do this in terms of years, but only in the day to day and often the hour to hour. Aging isn't a choice. It just happens. And, unfortunately, it isn't always the "Golden Years" or the years don't have as much gold in them as we thought or hoped.

With each new pain and ache, don't become negative. Rather, celebrate the life God has given you. How we respond to these aches will determine how we grow old.

* * * * *

Father God, let me enjoy each day as if it were my last. Let my eyes see Your beauty in nature and let my nose smell the fragrance of Your flowers. Each day is all I have. Help me appreciate it in You. Amen.

Interview Your Friends

A man of too many friends comes to ruin, but there is a friend who sticks closer than a brother.

PROVERBS 18:24

A good paraphrase of today's Scripture is: "A woman of too many friends will be broken into pieces. Indiscriminately chosen friends may bring trouble, but a genuine friend sticks with you through thick and thin." Our friends have a positive or negative effect on our lives. As parents, we know that, and many of us have told our children to be careful who they run with because people are known by the company they keep. There are areas in our lives that keep us from choosing who we are around, such as work, church, neighbors, and social clubs. In these settings, we are thrown together. However, within our family and in our private times, we can be very discerning about the people we associate with. We need to realize that our time and energy are among our most precious assets. Therefore, it's important to make wise choices in our selection of people we spend time with. Do they build us up and encourage us to be better than we would be by ourselves?

Why have you chosen the people who are closest to you? How do they contribute to who you are? I'm not saying that you should cast off those people who don't contribute positively to your life, but you might evaluate their part in contributing to who you are. I encourage you to notice how you respond when you are around certain people. Do you respect them? Do they encourage you to grow? Do you have kindred spirits? Do you share like values? If you can't answer to the affirmative, you might want to consider how much time you want to spend with them. Some changes might be in order.

You have a limited amount of time to spend with others, so select wisely. Much of who you are—positive as well as negative—will be influenced by the friends you keep.

. . . . .

God, thank You for the wonderful group of friends I have. You have brought into my life such a great support system. Even though I can't give each friend equal time, they are there supporting me in daily prayer. I appreciate how You have screened out negative influences and encourage me to spend time with those who love me and lift me up. Amen.

Friendship

*A friend loves at all times, and a
brother is born for adversity.*

Proverbs 17:17

I have been so blessed with great friendships. By the grace of God I've accumulated so many; at times they seem like puppies hanging around a food bowl. They each have brought such tenderness to my life and the joy of great anticipation for when we meet. Some friends just want to curl up around me and cozy up on a warm blanket and enjoy the strokes I give them. In return, they give me the nudge of their noses that tells me they so enjoy our time together. On occasion, I have even given my friends time to doze on the couch, and when they awaken we continue our time together. Friends are so warm and cuddly.

Henry Wadsworth Longfellow wrote a poem that expresses the true love of friends and how they linger over a period of years:

> I shot an arrow into the air,
> It fell to earth, I knew not where;
> For, so swiftly it flew, the sight
> Could not follow it in its flight.

I breathed a song into the air,
It fell to earth, I knew not where;
For who has sight so keen and strong,
That it can follow the flight of song?

Long, long afterward, in an oak
I found the arrow, still unbroke;
And the song, from beginning to end,
I found again in the heart of a friend.

* * * * *

Lord, what would I do without all my friends? They give me such support and strength. They are part of what gives my day purpose. May I be a friend to my friends. Thank You for friendships. Amen.

You Are Known by Your Choices

If any of you lacks wisdom, let him ask of God,
who gives to all generously and without reproach,
and it will be given to him.

JAMES 1:5

I used to tell the women who attended my seminars that there are three things that determine what each of us will be in five years:

- ❧ the people we meet
- ❧ the books we read
- ❧ the choices we make

I liked to emphasize the third one because so often we forget how our choices have such a significant impact on us, our lives, and the lives of our loved ones.

The choices we make determine who we are now and who we will be in the future. The more wisdom we have the better choices we will make. I have found that any wisdom I may have is that which I gained from reading and studying the holy Scriptures. Anything else I consider "knowledge." Knowledge is much easier and faster to acquire than wisdom. Gaining wisdom is a lifelong pursuit and cannot be attained in a college class or through a search on the Internet.

The Bible is full of wonderful assurances and promises for all who believe in Jesus Christ, the Son of God. But people must *choose Jesus* as their own Savior before they can claim these promises personally. How can these promises be yours? The Bible says to:

> *Recognize* you cannot be saved by trying to be good, or because you are doing the best you can, or because you are a member of a specific social or religious organization. God says we are not saved by our good works: "By grace you have been saved through faith; and that not of yourselves, it is the gift of God; not as a result of works, so that no one may boast" (Ephesians 2:8-9).

> *Confess* that you cannot save yourself. Confess that you are a guilty sinner worthy of God's righteous judgment, and that you are hopelessly lost without the Lord Jesus Christ as your personal Savior. "If we confess our sins, he is faithful and just and will forgive us our sins and purify us from all unrighteousness" (1 John 1:9 NIV).

> *Believe* the Good News that Jesus died for the ungodly. He also died for you and settled your sin debt by His death on Calvary's cross. Believe the blessed news that Christ was raised from the dead and now lives to save all who will come to Him in faith. "God demonstrates His own love toward us, in that while we were yet sinners, Christ died for us. Much more then, having now been justified by His blood, we

shall be saved from the wrath of God through Him. For if while we were enemies we were reconciled to God through the death of His Son, much more, having been reconciled, we shall be saved by His life" (Romans 5:8-10).

Call on the name of the Lord Jesus Christ with a sincere desire to be saved from your sins. "Everyone who calls on the name of the Lord will be saved" (Romans 10:13 NIV).

Rely on God's sure promises, not on your feelings. By faith declare you are saved by the blood of Jesus Christ, shed for the forgiveness of your sins. Openly confess Him as your Lord and Savior. Jesus said, "Whoever acknowledges me before others, I will also acknowledge before my Father in heaven" (Matthew 10:32).

If you have never put your faith in Jesus as your personal Savior, I encourage you to do it right now!

· · · · ·

Gracious Lord, I realize I'm a sinner and separated from You. I open my heart to receive You as my personal Savior and Lord of my life. I know You will forgive me of my sins. I want You to be my Mentor. Give me Your guidance and purpose for my life. I want You to be the Potter, and I will be Your clay. Mold me into who You want me to be. Amen.

Be Still, My Soul

Wear my yoke—for it fits perfectly—and
let me teach you; for I am gentle and humble,
and you shall find rest for your souls;
for I give you only light burdens.
MATTHEW 11:29 TLB

We make a big mistake if we forget to calm our spirits and seek the stillness we need to walk peacefully in this crazy world. God, speaking through the psalmist, urges us, "Be still, and know that I am God" (Psalm 46:10 NIV). Easier said than done, right? Let me urge you today in the strongest possible terms: Do whatever it takes to nurture stillness in your life. Don't let the enemy wear you so thin that you lose your balance and perspective. Regular time for stillness is as important and necessary as sleep, exercise, and nutritious food.

So what's the secret to making time you need for yourself? First, be realistic about what this will look like. You don't have to invest a large block of time. Fifteen minutes here and there can do wonders. Next, make yourself unavailable to the rest of the world for a few moments each day. Be available to God, to yourself, and then, ultimately, to others. Turn off your cell phone and have all calls go to voice mail.

· · · · ·

Father God, help me remember that You came to the world in a simple manger to a simple man and woman. You came simply to love us. All You ask of me is a simple response. Amen.

Say "Yes" for Tomorrow

*Rejoice that your names are
recorded in heaven.*

LUKE 10:20

A few days after Roy Rogers passed away at his home in Apple Valley, California, a local Christian television station ran a tribute to his life. One of the segments had Dale Evans, Roy's wife, singing a song entitled "Say 'Yes' for Tomorrow." This song was dedicated to the memory of Roy's early decision to put his trust in Jesus as his Savior. While listening to this song, I thought back over my life, back to when I invited Jesus as my Lord into my heart. At that time I made the most important decision in my life. I truly said yes for tomorrow in that I settled my eternity by saying yes to Jesus. I was a 16-year-old who came from a Jewish background. Even though my decision for Christ didn't set well with my extended family of aunts and uncles, it did settle for me what my tomorrows would be. My direction for the future was decided. As I've matured, I've realized that many adults have never made that affirmation. What a shame to search all one's life and then, at the end of life, be unsure of what the future might hold.

If you haven't settled what tomorrow will be like, take time today to guarantee your destination. Confirm to your family that you will be united together forever in heaven by accepting Jesus Christ and sharing His love with them.

* * * * *

Great Provider, I thank You for providing a way so I can know where my tomorrows will be. Thank You for sending Jesus to pay the price on the cross for my sins. I'm so glad I said yes to Him! Amen.

A Gift of Tea

*Always seek after that which is good for
one another and for all people.*
1 THESSALONIANS 5:15

What better gift can you give someone than a little bit of relaxation and peace of mind? I believe that tea provides that perfect respite for anyone. I am becoming more of a tea person each day I live. I love the beauty and simplicity of teatime. One of the nicest things about discovering the beauty of tea is that I get my Bob to enjoy a steaming cup of tea with me. Since he enjoys having a pot of tea in the afternoon, I've been able to delight in this great tradition.

Tea is a great gift idea for anyone of any age. Tea's popularity makes it easy to find gifts in all sizes and price ranges—from teacups or teapots to scone mixes and lovely teas of different origins and flavors. Tea makes a lovely hostess gift, and the recipient will be touched by your thoughtfulness.

After one of those days that seems to go on forever, take a break, sit back, set aside just a little bit of time for yourself, and relax with a delicious cup of tea. Hot or iced, you will discover this is the way to experience comfort and serenity wherever you are.

In a fast-moving world, we must take time to refresh ourselves. Nothing works better than a short break from your daily routine to stop, sip, and be still.

• • • • •

Dear God, thanks for reminding me that I need to take a break from the routines of the day and refresh myself with a break called tea. Amen.

It's Okay to Be Selfish

You shall love your neighbor as yourself.
LEVITICUS 19:18

One thing that I notice about so many people is they are burned out because they spend so much time serving others and take no time for themselves. As a young mom, I was going from sun-up to late in the evening just doing the things moms do. When evening came around, I was exhausted. All I wanted to do was take a hot bath and slip into bed to catch as much sleep as possible before I was awakened in the night by one of the children. Yes, my Bob helped, but there were certain things Mom had to do.

After several years of this, I remember thinking, "I've got to have some time just for me. I need help." One of the things I did was to get up a half hour before everyone else so I could spend time in the Scriptures over an early cup of tea. This one activity had an incredibly positive effect upon my outlook. I went on to make arrangements to get my hair and nails taken care of periodically. I was even known to purchase a new outfit (on sale, of course) occasionally. As I matured, I discovered that I became a better parent and wife when I set aside time for me and had my emotional tank filled up. After that, I had plenty of love and care left over to share with my loved ones.

When you are able to spend some time just for you, you will be more relaxed and your family and home will function better. The following "selfish" rituals don't have to be long in duration. Sometimes short experiences pay big dividends. I find these to be beneficial time-outs:

- taking a cozy, warm bath with bath salts and a flickering candle
- getting a massage
- having my hair and nails done
- meeting a friend for lunch
- listening to my favorite CD
- reading a good book
- writing a poem
- getting cozy on the couch
- watching a classic movie

· · · · ·

Father, I want time for me in such a big way, but I always thought it was selfish. Thanks for reminding me that it's okay to take time for me regularly. I know I will be more loving to those around me after I've rested and spent time with You. Amen.

Live Life on Purpose

Whether you eat or drink or whatever you do,
do it all for the glory of God.
1 CORINTHIANS 10:31 NIV

Have you ever been challenged to live life "on purpose"? If not, I challenge you now. God has placed us here on earth for a reason. And when we discover that reason and live our lives to that godly end, we find true satisfaction.

I've been very fortunate to meet a lot of wonderful people. All walks of life, all colors, all denominations, and some with no denominations. But the ones I count the most wise are those who understand that everything is to be done to the glory of God. They directed their lives toward a purpose—and that simple difference has given them the impetus and energy to succeed where many others have failed.

In ancient days, the craftsmen, artisans, and musicians proclaimed their godly purpose in life by what they produced. That's why the great classics of the world reflect a spiritual tribute to who God is. Through their endeavors, their work was beautiful and thus eternal.

In the twenty-first century, few artists are creating works that will attain "classic" status. Why? Because most composers, sculptors, writers, and artists don't create their works to glorify God. Often what was once ugly is now considered beautiful, and what was beautiful has become ugly. Just look at the contemporary music, art, theater, cinema, and literature to see how far we have strayed.

God's desire is for you and each member of your family to be purposeful human beings. To work toward meaningful goals and experience the joy of achievement. So learn to live your life on purpose, and teach your children to do the same. If necessary, write out some obtainable goals and work toward them. Read books that motivate you toward your goals or that help you set worthy goals. Above all, pray for God's guidance for your "on purpose" life.

. . . . .

Creator, give me purposeful direction for living a life that will glorify You. I'm tired of "shooting from the hip." I'm weary of coasting. Help me choose wisely and move toward the goals You want me to achieve. Amen.

Inspiration for Your Quiet Moments

🌺 🌺 🌺

Quiet-time Quilt

*D*oesn't everyone love the comfort of a special blanket or quilt? If you don't have one…find one or make one. Review your closet's inventory and rediscover a fuzzy fleece you usually only bring out when guests have arrived or the holidays approach. Let this be your marker for your special place of quiet for the next day. Before you go to bed or as soon as you rise, drape your "comfort" quilt over the chaise, the desk chair, or that large floor pillow you love. This will remind you to come back soon to this place of cozy peace to be with God and your thoughts. This is especially wonderful during the chillier months. An added bonus? The blanket can always be your reminder that God has you covered!

Be a Woman of Trust

*Trust in the LORD with all your heart and lean not on
your own understanding; in all your ways submit to
him, and he will make your paths straight.*

PROVERBS 3:5-6 NIV

I've heard husbands and wives discuss how difficult
it is for them to trust one another. While many couples might depend on one another, they struggle to trust
their spouse enough to work toward common goals. Are
they stubborn, mean, uncaring, or apathetic? No. These are
good folks who have forgotten a key factor in their relationship. They are supposed to be *trusting God* in every situation.
That is how a couple can work toward a common objective,
a purposed life together, and a faithful relationship.

When you and your husband truly begin working
together as a team, you can accomplish so much more than
you could ever accomplish alone. Sometimes I need a masculine point of view, and sometimes Bob needs to see the
feminine viewpoint. We balance out each other. I'm a better
woman because of him, and he's a better man because of me.
I don't have his strengths, and he doesn't have my strengths.
We've learned to let each other achieve satisfaction and success in our areas of strength.

One of the things I do in our marriage is let Bob know I
appreciate all the ways he protects our family. Through the

years I've affirmed him in that role. But as with most valuable truths, I had to learn to do that. Let me share an example. Early in our marriage, we lived near a busy intersection with no stoplights. We had to negotiate it every day. Trying to turn onto that busy thoroughfare from our street made a nervous wreck out of me. The cars came so fast—from both directions—and we had to merge quickly with speeding traffic. To make the left turn we needed, we often had to wait a long time for appropriate gaps in the traffic.

I admit that I'm a more cautious driver than Bob. And in situations where I would typically wait for a better opening, he stomped on the accelerator and darted into the flow of traffic. Frankly, it scared me, and I used to grip the passenger side armrest and close my eyes tightly when he took off. We never had any real problems or accidents related to Bob's quick-reflex driving style, but it frightened me—and I told him so.

Finally, after weeks of this, it dawned on me that I was basically telling him I didn't trust him. So I swallowed hard and resolved to change my behavior at that intersection the next time we approached it. And that's just what I did. Instead of tensing up and looking quickly back and forth or closing my eyes, I forced myself to relax and leave the driving and my fate in Bob's hands.

After he slipped the car smoothly into what looked to me like an incredibly small gap in traffic, I said nothing, trying to be the very picture of relaxation and ease. I'll always remember that moment. Bob shot me a quick glance and said, "Well? You didn't say anything to me this time."

I replied, "You know, honey, I trust you."

"Hmmm," was all he said. But I could see my words had an effect. There have been other situations in driving when I saw things one way and he saw things in another, and because he was driving, we went with his instincts rather than mine. Yes, sometimes it's very difficult to sit there, trust him, and submit to his decision making. But that is exactly what God asks me to do as his wife.

If we can't yield to our husband's leadership in small situations, how obedient will we be to God in really big situations? This doesn't imply that as wives we're inferior to our husbands in any way. No, it simply means God established a certain hierarchy or chain of command in the family, and He promised to bless those who obey His Word.

⋆ ⋆ ⋆ ⋆ ⋆

Father God, may I turn my heart to You and walk in all Your ways and keep Your commands with a willing heart. Amen.

You Will Smile Again

O my soul, why be so gloomy and discouraged? Trust in
God! I shall again praise him for his wondrous help; he
will make me smile again, for he is my God!
PSALM 43:5 TLB

There were times when I didn't think I would smile or
laugh again. Today's verse was one that often brought
cheer to my heart. "He will make me smile again." Don't you
just love that? When my spirit becomes gloomy, I choose to
continually trust in God. Christ does not force our will to
bend to His; He only receives what we give Him.

Despite what's happening in our lives, we can say loud
and clear, "I will not fear!" Time and time again, God has
given us confidence that we can believe Him for the future.
He is our refuge and strength. Pretty simple, isn't it?

Quite often now, a smile will sneak across my face during a hard day. It feels so good to smile. It's as if my body and
heart take a smile as a sign to relax and experience the joys,
especially the small, simple ones. Smiling is one of the most
therapeutic exercises we can do.

When a sickness, challenge, or loss starts to consume
your thoughts, ease your lips into a smile. In time, this will
become a second-nature response and will reflect your confidence in the Lord to provide, comfort, and accompany you
at all times.

· · · · ·

God, grant me the desire and will to smile. I love to share a smile with others and to receive one back. May others see You through my smile. Amen.

Lift Yourself Up

You formed my inward parts; You wove me in my mother's womb. I will give thanks to You, for I am fearfully and wonderfully made; wonderful are Your works, and my soul knows it very well.

PSALM 139:13-14

"If only I could have a straight nose, a tummy tuck, blond hair, larger (or smaller) breasts, or be more like so-and-so, I would be okay as a person." Have you heard this? Said this? I rarely hear women talk about how satisfied they are with how God made them.

"God must have made a mistake when He made me." "I'm certainly the exception to His model creation." "There's so much wrong with me, I'm discouraged about everything." These negative thoughts poison our system. We can't be lifted up when we spend so much time tearing ourselves down. When we are in negative mode, we can always find verification for what we're looking for. If we concentrate on the negative, we lose sight of all the positive aspects of our lives. We justify our damaging assumptions when we overlook the good God has for us.

These critical vibes create more negative vibes. Soon we are in a downward spiral. When we concentrate on our imperfections, we have a tendency to look at what's wrong and not what's right. Putting ourselves down can have some severe personal consequences.

Have you ever realized that God made you uniquely different from everyone else? (Even if you're a twin, you are different.) Yes, it is important to work on improving your imperfections, but don't dwell on them so much that you forget who you are in the sight of God. The more positive you are toward yourself, the more you will grow into the person God had in mind when He created you. Go easy on yourself. Remember, none of us will ever be perfect. The only way we will improve our self-image is by being positive and acknowledging that we are God's creation. Negativity tears down; positivity builds up.

* * * * *

Father, You knew me while I was in my mother's womb. I hunger to be the woman You created me to be. Help me become all You had in mind for me. Cut off my negative thoughts and expressions. I want people around me to know me as a positive person. I want to reflect Your love. Amen.

Don't Forget the Past

From infancy you have known the Holy Scriptures,
which are able to make you wise for salvation
through faith in Christ Jesus.
2 TIMOTHY 3:15 NIV

How many of us have lamented things in our past? Sometimes we meet people who dwell on the past so much it's as if they live there permanently. We all have actions, words, mistakes, and sins that blemish our personal histories, but we mustn't forget that when we know and love the Lord, our past is an amazing miracle because it brought us to the place of faith we stand in today.

God knows your past, including your long or short list of transgressions, but what He sees is the new creation you are through His Son Jesus Christ. What He notices is your faithfulness now and your desire to follow Him. God has loved you and known you from the very beginning, and He's just as excited over you as He was the day He created you. You and I are here today—and not by accident. We are here for a purpose. Have you taken time to consider what that purpose might be?

In Scripture, we are challenged not to forget what matters most. Paul writes in 2 Timothy 1:6-7, "I remind you to kindle afresh the gift of God which is in you through the laying on of my hands. For God has not given us a spirit of timidity, but of power and love and discipline."

In these latter days, we believers will be called on to stand up and give witness to Jesus and what He has done through history. We are told that during the last days people will...

- ignore God
- love possessions and things
- use other people
- play religious games
- be boastful and proud
- see children being disobedient to parents
- be ungrateful
- consider nothing sacred

This is certainly a list that seems appropriate for today. Every day I try to remember the lessons of history to remind myself...

- to follow the examples God has given: "You know what I believe and the way I live and what I want. You know my faith in Christ and how I have suffered. You know my love for you, and my patience" (2 Timothy 3:10 TLB).

- to remain in God's Word: "The whole Bible was given to us by inspiration from God and is useful to teach us what is true and to make us realize

267

what is wrong in our lives; it straightens us out and helps us do what is right" (2 Timothy 3:15 TLB).

🌿 to complete my calling: "'As surely as I live,' says the Lord, 'every knee will bow before me; every tongue will acknowledge God.' So then, each of us will give an account of ourselves to God" (Romans 14:11-12 NIV).

Biblical history lets me rest assured that God has a master plan for all of history, including mine. Though we might not know His master plan, we do know God's thoughts are bigger than our thoughts. I'm not capable of understanding every event in history, but because I know who God is, I can be at peace with all situations.

·   ·   ·   ·   ·

Dear God, give me a desire to know my history so I can better understand the present and trust You even more for my future. Give me a desire to reach out and find my purpose in life. Amen.

The Wise Are Mature

We are no longer to be children, tossed here and there
by waves and carried about by every wind of doctrine,
by the trickery of men, by craftiness in deceitful
scheming; but speaking the truth in love, we are
to grow up in all aspects into Him.

EPHESIANS 4:14-15

God does not want us to remain spiritually immature. Many of the 30- to 50-year-old women I meet seem to dwell on how old they are. They don't seem to believe there is much hope or time for them to make more of an impact in life. I always reassure them how beautiful the older decades are. Each season of life has so much to offer. Life becomes richer the more mature we become.

In our Christian walk, we are encouraged not to remain as babes and children, but to wean ourselves off spiritual milk and soft food and grow into healthier foods. God wants us to exhibit signs of maturity, and many times this comes through very difficult life situations. My experience validates that we grow through difficulties, not just through the good times.

If we are not mature, the reason is observable: We have not been workers but idlers in our study of the Bible. Those who are just "Sunday Christians" will never grow to maturity. It takes the study of the Scriptures to become meat-eaters of God's Word. We must be workers in the Scriptures. We must roll up our sleeves and do the job of investigation ourselves instead of expecting a pastor or teacher to do it for us.

Immersing yourself in the stillness with God is doing the work of maturing your walk. And the best part is that it feels like a luxury. But don't let that fool you, my friend. Your time with the Lord is your way to grow in faith, belief, wisdom, and love.

• • • • •

Father God, thank You for inspiring men of old to write Your Scriptures. They have become my Scriptures; they have led to my salvation. Without the knowledge found in Your Book, my life would be tossed about like the waves in the wind. Thank You for my stability. Amen.

Time to Celebrate

Say thank you to the Lord for being so good,
for always being so loving and kind.
PSALM 107:1 TLB

Make celebrations a tradition in your family. Why? Life is for the living! There's always something to celebrate. Just because you are in a difficult fight for renewed health or to get through a tough situation doesn't mean you have to stop celebrating. To the contrary, now is when you really want to enjoy all those important events in life.

Celebrate everything—good days, bad days that are finally over, birthdays, and even non-birthdays! Get the whole family involved preparing for a dinner celebration. Make it special. Let the children make place cards, set the table, help you cook, and create a beautiful, creative centerpiece.

Take time to honor the people in your family and in your life. Listen to one another. Share meals. Celebrate the big and small events that shape a life. This is a way to share God's goodness and to model an example of His love to your family and friends. Let your celebration sharing extend beyond the family. Several times a year, create a "love basket" filled with food for a needy family. Or try spending part of your holidays helping out at a shelter or mission.

Don't limit yourself. Look for ways to celebrate your many blessings.

* * * * *

Father God, there are many reasons to celebrate life today. Let me be a helper for those who want to celebrate but don't know how. Amen.

If Only

*When a man is gloomy, everything seems
to go wrong; when he is cheerful,
everything seems right!*
PROVERBS 15:15 TLB

We all know that gloom brings doom, but we still tend to concentrate on the negatives. How many times have you said "If only"?

If only…I didn't have this illness.

If only…I could win the lottery.

If only…I had a better job.

If only…my husband made more money.

If only…my husband was a Christian.

If only…my son wouldn't run around with that person.

If only…my parents were still alive.

If only…if only…if only.

This list could go on and on. The "if onlys" of our lives prevent us from being the people God wants us to be. We get caught in a mindset that prevents us from turning our lives around.

Your friends won't stick around if all they hear from you are "if onlys." Your conversation drains the life from those around you. Instead of saying "if only," try "I can!"

. . . . .

God, I know You don't want to hear my "if onlys."
Help me be upbeat and bury my negative attitude.
Amen.

Inspiration for Your Quiet Moments

❧ ❧ ❧

Walk and Talk with God

Is there a stretch of bike path, neighborhood sidewalk, or hiking trail near you? These are invitations to spend time walking and talking to God. It is amazing how once we start moving, the prayer needs and ideas seem to shift within and soon we don't want to stop lifting up our dreams and concerns and hopes. Many women use their walking time to pray for the people in the houses they pass and for everyone else God brings to their thoughts.

It is a joy and privilege to pray for acquaintances and strangers. You don't know what is going on in their lives, but God does. Lift up their unnamed needs, challenges, and hopes. The next time you see these people—the mail carrier, the boy raking leaves in front of the yellow house, the elderly woman watering her geraniums—you'll feel the deep delight of having prayed for God's precious children.

Leave a Legacy

I am mindful of the sincere faith within you, which
first dwelt in your grandmother Lois and your mother
Eunice, and I am sure that it is in you as well.

2 Timothy 1:5

Have you ever been challenged regarding what kind of legacy you are going to leave to your heirs? We all leave some type of belief system, regardless of how we live our lives. It will either be good and positive or it will be bad and negative. Our heirs will reflect what kind of influence we have on their lives. Paul writes a second letter to his friend Timothy and challenges him to remember the influence that his mother and grandmother had on his life. The apostle encourages Timothy to concentrate on the past, present, and future aspects of developing a legacy. Paul wants Timothy—and us—to "fan the flame" of faith for God. The character development we need is to embrace and live out the fact that God has not given us a spirit of timidity (cowardice) but one of power, love, and discipline.

The second part of the legacy Paul advocates is to follow the plan God has given us. The apostle warned Timothy that at times he might have to suffer for preaching the gospel. He stressed not to be ashamed, but to believe and be convinced that Jesus is able to guard what was entrusted to Him by God, including the people who choose to believe in Him. That's essential for us to do too.

Another aspect of passing the legacy of faith to others is to pattern our lives from what we have seen. Paul stressed that we retain the standard of sound words we learn from him. We are to guard, through the Holy Spirit, the treasure, the gospel, that has been entrusted to us.

The last aspect of developing a worthwhile legacy is to pass it on. Paul told Timothy to entrust these truths to "faithful men who will be able to teach others also." Be a mom who cares about the kind of legacy you leave when the Lord calls you home. Teach your children these truths:

- Fan the flame of passion for God.
- Follow God's plan for you.
- Pattern your life from what you learn in God's Word.
- Pass the wisdom of Scriptures on to those around you and those who will follow.

* * * * *

Holy God, I want to pass on a godly legacy—one that upholds the tenets of the gospel of Jesus Christ. Let me begin today to take life—and You—more seriously than I ever have. Amen.

Always Be

Always be joyful. Always keep on praying.
No matter what happens, always be thankful,
for this is God's will for you who
belong to Christ Jesus.

1 THESSALONIANS 5:16-18 TLB

If the Bible says it, I believe it. That's a good slogan to live by—as long as we go beyond just believing with our minds and begin to obey with our lives. The Bible means what it says, and that's important to keep in mind. Today's verses tell us to *always* be joyful, *always* keep praying, *always* be thankful. Most of us manage to be joyful, to pray, to be thankful sometimes—but always? That's tough. But when God says *always*, He means always! For God's people, joy, prayer, and thanksgiving are to be constants. We're supposed to stay simple and pure before the Lord and live out these three attributes of the Christian life consistently. We can't do all this without God's help, of course. But that's the heart of the Good News. God is always with us. When we do live this way, we not only experience the full flow of God's blessing, but we reflect those blessings to the world around us.

Remember, you might be the only Bible some people will ever read.

• • • • •

Father God, flowers, colors, textures, rain, sunshine, water, soil—You are the wonderful creator of everything. Produce and establish Your love and goodness in me so I can share it with those around me. Amen.

The Secret of the Wise Man

Behold, You desire truth in the innermost being, and in the hidden part You will make me know wisdom.

Psalm 51:6

I was driving down one of the busy freeways in Southern California when a sign suddenly appeared before me that read, "What the fool does at the end, wise men do at the beginning." I don't know how I was able to glimpse this since I was driving by, but my mind affirmed that this slogan has so much meaning.

We live in a day when humanity has sold out to secular materialism, a day when many people have put God on hold. The attitude of "I can do it myself! I don't need help from anyone—especially from a God I can't see or touch!" rules. But as time goes by, many older people seem to get more wisdom after they have found that their life paths have given them little meaning in life. As they ponder mortality, they often realize that the simplicity of their youth offered a peace and meaning that they rejected. Wise people, on the other hand, have adopted the fear of God at a young age. They have studied the wisdom of Scripture and applied it to their value structure.

Wisdom comes from knowing God and understanding His will for our lives. The Holy Spirit assists us in our quest for wisdom by enabling us to view the world as God perceives it. From an early age we can seek God's wisdom. We don't have to wait until we are old to figure out this puzzle called life. In Psalm 111:10 we read, "The fear of the LORD is the beginning of wisdom; a good understanding have all those who do His commandments; His praise endures forever."

Don't put off until tomorrow what you can do today. A wasted lifetime is a shame. Go to the cross of Jesus and trust Him with the simplicity of childlike faith.

· · · · ·

Faithful Lord, I don't want to wait until I'm old to exhibit Your trait of wisdom. I want a life of trusting You and Your Word. May I also be able to transmit this faith and wisdom to my family. Bless me as I put my faith in Your hands. Amen.

Have Pleasant Dreams

When you lie down, you will not be afraid;
when you lie down, your sleep will be sweet.
Do not be afraid of sudden fear nor of the onslaught
of the wicked when it comes; for the
Lord will be your confidence and will keep
your foot from being caught.
PROVERBS 3:24-26

Do you ever have trouble sleeping? I know there can be plenty of nights that you might toss and turn. You just can't relax because you're thinking about tomorrow's schedule. You've got to do this, and you've got to do that. When will it end? Wow! There's a lot to be concerned about. However, today's verse tells us that we can lie down without fear and even have pleasant dreams. God protects us even as we sleep. In fact, when we are quiet and gently submitting our lives to Him, I am sure He can get even more done on our behalf!

You don't have to count sheep to fall asleep. Just remember that God knows all about your tomorrows. He has gone ahead of you to smooth out the rough patches. Whatever is troubling you, He already knows all about it. And if you are awaiting news or details or anticipating how life will unfold, remember that God has that all in His hands as well.

God is with you today and will be with you tomorrow. Let Him handle the details tonight as you lay your head on the pillow. Night night!

• • • • •

Father, I want to be content with whatever You choose to provide. Give me the grace to let the rest go and trust You for my every need. Amen.

Our Sweet Refuge

You are my hiding place; You preserve me from trouble;
You surround me with songs of deliverance.

PSALM 32:7

My experiences in life have confirmed that God is truly my hiding place. He is closer than a brother, and one to whom I can go in all phases of life. While you and I make homes for our families and strive to do right by them and by God, it is truly by God's grace that we have strength for what comes our way. We can pull God's grace around ourselves like a soft blanket against winter's chill. There is refuge and delight in His sweet presence. My friend, I hope that each day presents many opportunities for you to go to the Lord and seek His comfort, direction, might, deliverance, and tenderness.

Women juggle so many responsibilities these days. It is important to prioritize because there are many times that we feel the burden to do more when God is asking us to do less—but do it with greater conviction and depth. Pay attention to the times when He nudges you to rest and reassess the priorities that influence your family members, other people in your life, and you. Do you realize your priorities can impact strangers? Friends you haven't met yet? A person across the globe even? You just don't know how God is going to use you when you are an open vessel for His goodness and love. I can assure you that it is a remarkable feeling each time you recognize God's touch in a situation, a conversation, or a decision.

For this moment, listen for the song of deliverance that is played for you. Let it ease your worries, calm your nerves, clear your perspective, and usher you to God's tender promises for your life today.

Lord, make me an instrument of your peace.

Where there is hatred, let me sow love;

Where there is injury, pardon;

Where there is doubt, faith;

Where there is despair, hope;

Where there is darkness, light;

and where there is sadness, joy.

St. Francis of Assisi

More Great Harvest House

Books by
Emilie and Bob Barnes

🌷 🌷 🌷

Emilie Barnes

101 Ways to Clean Out the Clutter

15 Minutes Alone with God

15 Minutes of Peace with God

15 Minutes with God for Grandma

The 15-Minute Organizer

365 Things Every Woman Should Know

365 Ways to Organize Everything
(with Sheri Torelli)

500 Time-Saving Hints for Every Woman

Friendship Teas to Go

Good Manners for Today's Kids

Good Manners in Minutes

A Grandma Is a Gift from God

Heal My Heart, Lord

If Teacups Could Talk

In the Stillness of Quiet Moments

An Invitation to Tea

A Journey Through Cancer

Keep It Simple for Busy Women

Let's Have a Tea Party!
(with Sue Christian Parsons)

A Little Book of Manners: Etiquette for Young Ladies
(with Anne Christian Buchanan)

A Little Princess in the Making

The Little Teacup That Talked

Meet Me Where I Am, Lord

Minute Meditations for Busy Moms

Minute Meditations for Healing & Hope

More Faith in My Day

More Hours in My Day
(with Sheri Torelli)

Quiet Moments Alone with God

Simple Secrets to a Beautiful Home

Survival for Busy Women

The Tea Lover's Devotional

The Twelve Teas of Inspiration

Walk with Me Today, Lord

You Are My Hiding Place, Lord

Youniquely Woman
(with Kay Arthur and Donna Otto)

Bob & Emilie Barnes

101 Ways to Love Your Grandkids

15-Minute Devotions for Couples

Good Manners for Today's Kids

A Little Book of Manners for Boys

Simple Secrets Couples Should Know

Together Moments for Couples

Bob Barnes

15 Minutes Alone with God for Men

500 Handy Hints for Every Husband

5-Minute Bible Workouts for Men

5-Minute Faith Builders for Men

Five Minutes in the Bible for Men

What Makes a Man Feel Loved